NORTH AFRICA

THE VEGETARIAN TABLE

NORTH AFRICA

THE VEGETARIAN TABLE

BY KITTY MORSE

PHOTOGRAPHY BY DEBORAH JONES

CHRONICLE BOOKS · SAN FRANCISCO

DEDICATION

To the wonderful cooks throughout the Maghreb
from whom I have learned so much

Library of Congress Cataloging-in-Publication Data:
Morse, Kitty.
The vegetarian table: North Africa/by Kitty Morse;
photography by Deborah Jones.
p. cm.
Includes index.
ISBN 0-8118-0694-4
1. Vegetarian cookery. 2. Cookery, North Africa. I. Title.
TS837.M73 1996
641.5′636—dc20 95-318331
CIP

Book Design: Louise Fili Ltd
Design Assistant: Tonya Hudson
Food Styling: Sandra Cook
Photo Styling: Sara Slavin
Photo Assistant: Jeri Jones
Food Styling Assistant: Allyson Levy

The photographer wishes to thank San Francisco stores
Zonal and F. Dorian, and Kitty and Owen Morse
for sharing their home and props.

Printed in Hong Kong.

Distributed in Canada by Raincoast Books,
8680 Cambie St., Vancouver, B.C. V6P 6M9

10 9 8 7 6 5 4 3 2 1

Chronicle Books
275 Fifth Street
San Francisco, CA 94103

CONTENTS

ACKNOWLEDGMENTS

❋

THIS BOOK IS, FOR ME, A WAY TO PERPETUATE THE MEMORY OF MY FATHER, CLIVE CHANDLER, M.B.E., AN ENGLISHMAN WHO ELECTED TO CALL CASABLANCA HOME FOR OVER FIFTY YEARS; I also want to honor the memory of my great-aunt Suzanne Coriat, Tita to her family, and also that of my great-grandmother, Maman Darmon, both natives of Algeria and long-time residents of Morocco, and both superb North African cooks. I am grateful for the precious contributions of my mother Nicole Darmon Chandler, my aunt Martine Darmon Meyer, my cousin Stephanie Meyer, and my brother Brian Patrick Chandler.

I owe a debt of gratitude to Tunis-born Moncef Jaziri and to his wife Swanli, who now make their home in San Diego. Thanks to them, the Jaziri family opened its doors to me in Gammarth, Tunisia. My heartfelt thanks to Fatma and Yamina Jaziri and to their lovely mother Meherzia, for a memorable Tunisian culinary experience. My gratitude also goes to Ahmed Henia and to the Ben Yedder family in Tunis; to the staff at the Sheraton Hotel in Hammamet; and especially to chef Ahmed Ouaili, who agreed to part with some of his favorite recipes.

Thanks to friends and colleagues Kim Upton and Jackie Shannon, for their invaluable editing input; to Pam Wischkaemper, Carole Bloom, Lily Loh, and Betz Collins, for providing moral support and encouragement while this project was taking shape; and to Susan Ciccone, for her linguistic assistance.

I want to thank Royal Air Maroc, the national airline of Morocco, and the staff of Olive Branch Tours in Casablanca for their kind assistance during my travels. Thanks to my friends Nadia and Aziz Belkasmi in Casablanca; to Bouchaib Marzouk, our wonderful cook and housekeeper, and to his wife Aicha in Azemmour, Morocco; to Hassania Bezzaz for sharing with me her knowledge of Berber lore and language; to transplanted Algerians Zoulikha Senoussaoui in Casablanca and Nacira Baba-Ahmed and Ghania Belbildia in Los Angeles; to my cousins Flor and Raph Scemama in Paris; and to Paris-based author Edmond Amran El Maleh, who hails from Essaouira, Morocco.

Thanks to Jim and Froukje Frost for sharing with me their intimate knowledge of Tunisia; to my agent Julie Castiglia; to my editors Bill LeBlond and Leslie Jonath; to photographer Deborah Jones; and a big thanks to all the tasters who helped evaluate innumerable variations of couscous, *tagines*, and *makhoudas* at our *kasbah* in Vista!

And to my husband Owen, whose keen observations and precious sense of humor helped me maintain the necessary focus, *Chokran! Merci!* Thank you!

INTRODUCTION

❂

"LA CUISINE, C'EST L'ÂME PARFUMÉE DE NOTRE CULTURE" ("CUISINE IS THE PERFUMED SOUL OF OUR CULTURE"), SAYS MOROCCAN-BORN WRITER EDMOND AMRAN EL MALEH. Its fragrance has thoroughly permeated the North African countries of Morocco, Tunisia, and Algeria, collectively known as the Maghreb, "the land where the sun sets," a name given to the region by medieval Arab historians. Here, the cuisine is redolent of exotic spices like saffron, ginger, and cinnamon, and vivid with the sun-drenched colors of a cornucopia of fresh fruits and vegetables available throughout the year, thanks to the region's mild Mediterranean climate. It is also a cuisine based on ancient traditions that have been handed down, most often orally, from mother to daughter.

Today, the foods of the Maghreb are generating intense interest among American culinary professionals, due in part to the increased awareness of the health benefits of the Mediterranean diet. Indeed, current research has shown that the peoples of the Mediterranean have one of the lowest incidences of heart disease in the world, leading nutritional experts to extol the virtues of a cuisine rich in fresh produce, legumes, cereals, pasta, and olive oil—all staples of the North African diet.

When a North African woman shops for her family at the city *marché* or at the open-air souk in the countryside, her basket overflows with the fruits and vegetables of the season, bunches of fresh herbs, fresh or dried fava beans, lentils, and of course, the pellets of cracked durum wheat, or semolina, called couscous. She will purchase meat, poultry, or fish mainly on special occasions, or when her finances allow. As John Buffa, an early nineteenth-century doctor, recounts in *Travels through the Empire of Morocco:* "The Moors (as Moroccans used to be known) in general, are extremely fond of vegetables, which contribute very much to their contentment. The peasants eat meat only on certain great days . . . and their favourite dish is cous-ca-sou [*sic*]."

This healthful diet, as well as the seductive seasonings that characterize the cuisine of the Maghreb, has always been part of my culinary repertoire. Growing up as I did in Dar Beida, the Arabic name for Casablanca, meant being exposed to a kaleidoscope of cultures. My high school classmates at the Lycée de Jeunes Filles, for instance, were not only of Moroccan descent, but also Tunisian, Algerian, French, Spanish, Portuguese, and Italian, to name a few. This cosmopolitan environment allowed me to become familiar with such diverse specialties as Tunisian *breiks,* Spanish churros, French cassoulet, Sephardic *dafina,* and of course, Moroccan couscous, which was, and still is, my favorite comfort food.

These dishes, among many others, evolved over centuries of cross-cultural exchanges with countries from all parts of the Mediterranean basin. When Phoenician sailors from the Levant first explored the North African coast around 1000 B.C., they encountered a population of indigenous Berbers who, some historians believe, had migrated from the Asian continent several thousand years earlier. These Berbers had already mastered the art of grafting the olive tree and lived for the most part on a diet of honey, fava beans, lentils, and wheat. It is they who many experts believe were the inventors of couscous.

While the Phoenicians were masters of trade (which included the precious saffron, used as a dye in Egypt since the time of the pharaohs), the Carthaginians developed a flourishing civilization based on agriculture. They established vast landholdings from the Cap Bon Peninsula east of Carthage all the way to the Atlantic coast in the west, and traded with caravans from as far away as the Sudan, on the southern edge of the Sahara. The Carthaginians also introduced new agricultural methods, greatly expanding the commercial cultivation of grapes, olives, wheat, and fruits.

The Romans, feeling increasingly threatened by Carthaginian expansion, laid siege to Carthage on two occasions and completely destroyed the city in 146 B.C. The Carthaginian territories became important provinces of the Roman empire, and provided so much of the Romans' food supply (over 60 percent of the empire's grain and much of its olive oil, according to documents of the period) that it became known as the bread basket of Rome. It remained so for almost five hundred years. The waning of Rome's domination of the Mediterranean in the fifth century provided an opportunity for expansion for northern European tribes such as the Vandals. They swept through Spain, eventually crossing into Morocco, before heading east to Carthage and on to Sicily, Corsica, and Sardinia. Their rule was to last over a century, during which time commercial activity with all parts of the Mediterranean continued to increase.

A fitful peace settled on North Africa until the beginning of the seventh century. At that time, Arab followers of the prophet Mohammed, fresh from their conquests in the eastern Mediterranean, introduced North Africa and the Maghreb to Islam, and to the culinary subtleties of Damascus, Baghdad, and Cairo. (These Moslem conquerors became known as the Moors, a word derived from Mauretania, the Roman name for the provinces of northwest Africa.) They crossed the Straits of Gibraltar to conquer Spain, where they remained until 1492. At that time, the Catholic monarchs of Spain gave an ultimatum to Moslems and Jews: Convert to Christianity, or be driven from the country.

Many chose exile rather than conversion. They took refuge in the Maghreb, bringing with them the rich traditions of El Andalus (the ancient name for the southwest region of Spain) and further broadening the cultural and culinary horizons of North Africa. The Spanish Moors settled in areas reminiscent of their former homeland, transforming towns like Fez in Morocco, Tlemcen in Algeria, and Tunis in Tunisia into vibrant gastronomic and architectural testaments to their elegant Andalusian and Moorish heritage. It is widely believed that these sophisticated exiles were responsible for introducing to the Maghreb the paper-thin pastry dough known today as *ouarka* in Morocco, *dioul* in Algeria, and *malsouka* in Tunisia. They also brought with them quinces, Valencia oranges, cherries, apricots, turnips, carrots, and eggplants, as well as potatoes, tomatoes, and chilies, which had been imported into Spain from the Americas by the conquistadores. Exotic spices like cumin, cinnamon, and cloves, a legacy of Portuguese spice traders, were also incorporated into North African cuisine. By the time the Ottomans invaded Tunisia and Algeria at the end of the sixteenth century, the inhabitants of the Maghreb were well versed in the pleasures of the table and eagerly adopted some of the refinements of Persian and Turkish cuisines.

The Ottomans were displaced by French colonizers in the early nineteenth century. These Pieds-Noirs (black feet), so called, according to local lore, because they wore heavy black boots, remained in the Maghreb until the middle of this century. (Originally, the term *Pied-Noir* referred only to the French settlers in Algeria, but has come to encompass those of Italian, Spanish, and Portuguese origin living anywhere in the Maghreb.) By the time Morocco, Algeria, and Tunisia regained their independence, many of the Pieds-Noirs who returned to France had adopted North African cuisine as their own. This contributed greatly to European cooks' acceptance of these exotic new flavors.

Like many Pieds-Noirs, my maternal grandfather was descended from Sephardic Jews who fled to North Africa following their expulsion from Spain at the time of the Inquisition. He emigrated with his family from the Algerian coastal city of Oran to Casablanca early in this century. This multicultural family background heavily influenced many of the recipes handed down to me by my great-grandmother. For Maman Darmon, as we called her, there was no greater pleasure than spending hours in the kitchen, planning and cooking the family meal. When I was growing up, I remember watching her by the hour in the kitchen of her spacious apartment in Casablanca, amid saucepans bubbling with simmering soups and baskets overflowing with fresh vegetables. She paid as much attention to details of presentation as she did to the painstaking preparation of the meal, heeding the wisdom of the Arab proverb: "First, you eat with your eyes."

Maman Darmon planned each of her meals as a series of seductions of the senses, first tantalizing the sense of sight, then the senses of smell and taste. As she dipped her spoon in a sauce, correcting the seasoning to her liking, exclamations of satisfaction in French, Spanish, and Arabic escaped her lips. When she set a heavy pan containing one of her specialties on the table and lifted the lid, she would be the first to inhale the heady scent of cinnamon, nutmeg, or mace. As the aromatic legacy of centuries of Sephardic culture wafted around the table, she would exclaim, eyes shining with delight: *"Ça sent bon! Vite! Passez-moi vos assiettes!"* ("It smells good! Quick! Hand me your plates!")

For this book, I have drawn heavily from my own collection of recipes. Many were given to me by members of my family and friends throughout the Maghreb. I call the dishes the names by which I have always known them. Because of my diverse family background, I refer to some by their Arabic name, others by their French, English, or Spanish name, and still others using a combination of two languages. I hope this repertoire of recipes will give your palate an exciting introduction to the exotic flavors of the perfumed soul of the culture of the Maghreb. *Bismillah! Bon appétit!*

DINING IN THE MAGHREB

ENTERTAINING, MOROCCAN STYLE

MOROCCANS, LIKE ALL NORTH AFRICANS, ARE RENOWNED FOR THEIR HOSPITALITY. THEY GO TO GREAT LENGTHS to see that every consideration is given to the comfort and enjoyment of their guests. To that end, they take the utmost care in preparing for a *diffa*, or banquet, where course after course of sumptuous dishes is served in such lavish quantities that you wonder who will eat all the food. The abundant display is a measure of the host's hospitality. Anything left over will go to feed members of the family and household staff not present at the banquet table.

Whenever I return to Morocco, I always look forward to attending a *diffa*. These banquets are held on special occasions such as weddings, births, or anniversaries of local saints. The *diffa* begins with a hand-washing ceremony, in which a young family member pours a stream of warm water over the outstretched hands of the guests and into an ornate copper basin. When their hands are dry, the member sprinkles them with a few fragrant drops of orange flower or rose water. The host then invokes Allah's blessing on the meal with one simple word: *Bismillah!* ("In the name of God!")

Chunks of warm bread are passed around to the guests as the first course begins, usually an assortment of exquisitely seasoned cooked or raw salads. After the salads, it is time for a golden *bastila*. The host first breaks the crisp, light crust with his fingers to let the steam escape from the layers of paper-thin *ouarka* (a dough much like Greek phyllo). After the pastry has cooled somewhat, guests break off pieces of the delicate bastila, filled with a mixture of shredded fowl, saffron, sugar, and ground almonds.

A savory *tagine* course usually follows the bastila. The word *tagine* applies to a luscious combination of meat, vegetables, or fruit, simmered in sauces redolent of cumin, saffron, or cinnamon. *Tagine* is also the name of the earthenware dish with a conical lid in which the stew is served. Dipping a piece of freshly baked bread into the rich sauce of a *tagine* is, for me, an unequaled dining pleasure.

After the *tagine* is cleared away, a mountain of steaming couscous crowned with vegetables and drizzled with broth is set in the center of the table. Guests make barely a dent in the bountiful dish, however, trying to save room for the fresh fruits, pastries, and mint tea that will be served for dessert.

DINING CUSTOMS

Most Algerians and Tunisians have long adopted Western-style tables and chairs, as well as Western dining utensils. Moroccans, however, favor handsomely carved sofas and hassocks set around low round tables. And many Moroccans still use the thumb and first two fingers of the right hand, along with chunks of fresh bread, to scoop up tender morsels from the communal dish. Guests are always offered the option of using silverware instead of their fingers.

SPECIAL INGREDIENTS AND EQUIPMENT

SPECIAL INGREDIENTS

ALMOND PASTE: A paste made of ground almonds and sugar, available in the baking section of most supermarkets.

BARLEY GRITS: This hulless cracked barley, called *belboula* in Morocco, has a coarser consistency and a nuttier flavor than couscous. You can find packages of instant barley grits in the cereal section of many natural foods stores, and in bulk in Middle Eastern markets. Prepare barley grits as you would couscous.

BHARAT: A seasoning blend made from dried rosebuds, cinnamon, and black pepper. It is used in Tunisia to flavor stews and egg dishes (see recipe on page 21).

CAPERS: These pickled buds of the *Capparis spinosa* are used extensively in Tunisian cuisine. They can be found in the gourmet section of supermarkets and in specialty foods stores. Pickled nasturtium buds are a less-expensive substitute for capers.

COUSCOUS: Boxes of instant medium-grain couscous are found in the pasta and rice section of most supermarkets. Couscous is also available in bulk in Middle Eastern markets and natural foods stores.

CUMIN: Ground cumin seed is one of the most commonly used spices in North African cuisine.

DRIED FAVA BEANS, GARBANZO BEANS, OR NAVY BEANS: Garbanzo beans (also called *ceci* beans, or chick-peas) and navy beans, both staples of Maghreb cuisine, are available canned or dried in supermarkets. Canned or dried fava beans are more commonly found in Middle Eastern food stores. See the method for soaking dried beans on page 24.

FOUL MUDAMMAS: Small brown-skinned fava beans are common in North Africa, where they are usually added to soups, or boiled and seasoned with cumin as an appetizer. *Foul mudammas* are available canned or dried in Middle Eastern markets. If you are using dried fava beans, follow the instructions on page 24 for soaking and cooking.

GROUND GINGER: An essential spice in North African cooking. Fresh ginger is not used, however.

HARISSA: A Tunisian hot sauce used to flavor North African dishes. Sometimes found in tubes or in cans in the specialty foods section of supermarkets, and in Middle Eastern markets (see recipe on page 19).

HROUSS: This specialty from Gabès, in the south of Tunisia, is a fiery paste made from sun-dried onions and chilies that are pounded to a paste and mixed with a variety of spices. Hrouss brings to mind *sambal*, a condiment used in Indonesian cuisine. *Sambal badjak* and *sambal manis*, which are blends of hot chilies and onions, are available in specialty markets or Asian markets. Use either of them as an alternative to *hrouss* or harissa.

MINT: Common backyard mint (*Mentha veridis*), used for mint tea. Tunisians prefer to make tea with dried peppermint leaves. The leaf is also ground to a powder and used as a flavoring for some meat dishes, Tunisian egg *tagines*, or soup. Dried peppermint has a stronger, more peppery flavor and is available in bulk in many natural foods stores.

NUTS: Almonds, pistachios, walnuts, and pine nuts are used extensively in desserts, as well as in savory dishes in North Africa. To toast nuts, see page 24.

OLIVE OIL: From a wide array of cooked or raw salads to succulent vegetable *tagines,* most of the dishes that characterize the cuisine of North Africa call for olive oil. The flavor and quality of olive oil is dependent on climate, soil, and irrigation, as well as on the environmental conditions at the time the olives were harvested. Olive oil is extracted from the fruit of the olive tree by pressing, without the use of chemicals. Grades of olive oil differ in aroma, flavor, color, and level of acidity. I prefer using extra-virgin olive oil, the fruitiest and highest grade of olive oil, especially in salad dressings, or when sautéing or browning foods. Research has shown that a diet high in monounsaturated fatty acids, like those found in olive oil, may help lower the LDL (so-called harmful cholesterol), while maintaining high levels of HDL (so-called good cholesterol), thus reducing some of the risk factors associated with heart disease.

OLIVES: Green, purple, and black olives are a staple of the North African diet. Their color depends upon the stage at which they are harvested. Green olives have the firmest flesh, as they are first to be picked. They are usually cured in brine and seasoned with dried herbs, hot peppers, or preserved lemon. They are the ones usually found in Moroccan *tagines.* As olives mature they turn purple, then black. In many dishes, purple and green olives such as Sicilian olives or diminutive French *picholine* are interchangeable. They are sometimes cracked to allow for better absorption of the flavorings. Black olives, on the other hand, are generally dry cured, meaning they are layered with salt until they shrivel and become chewy. Most black Moroccan olives are cured in this manner, as are French Nyons olives. The more commonly available brine-cured Greek Kalamata olives make good substitutes. Black olives are generally served alone as appetizers, or used to garnish salads. To store brine-cured olives, keep them covered with their brine in an airtight container in the refrigerator. (See page 156 for sources of Middle Eastern olives.)

ORANGE FLOWER WATER: Distilled from orange blossoms, this fragrant water is used throughout the Maghreb to flavor pastries, desserts, and beverages. In the United States, orange flower water (also called orange blossom water) is found in supermarkets and large liquor stores, as well as in Middle Eastern markets and specialty foods stores.

PAPRIKA, SWEET OR HOT: A common spice in North African cuisine. In Morocco, hot paprika is usually added according to individual taste.

PARSLEY, FLAT-LEAF (ITALIAN): This particular variety of parsley, which has broad, flat leaves and an intense fragrance, is used throughout North Africa. It is commonly available in American supermarkets.

PHYLLO DOUGH: This paper-thin Greek pastry dough is a good substitute for *dioul, ouarka,* or *malsouka.* You can find phyllo dough in the frozen foods section of supermarkets. Fresh phyllo dough is also sold by some Greek markets, especially in larger cities. To thaw frozen phyllo, place it in the refrigerator overnight, or let it sit at room temperature for 2 hours.

ROSE WATER: Available in Middle Eastern markets, in large supermarkets, and sometimes in pharmacies.

ROSE GERANIUM WATER: Distilled from the petals of wild rose-scented geraniums, this fragrant water is used to flavor desserts and pastries in Tunisia. It is not commonly available in the United States. Use rose water as a substitute.

SAFFRON: Spanish saffron, the dried stigmas of the *Crocus sativus,* is the world's most expensive spice. In minute quantities, it imparts its distinctive aroma to some Moroccan and Algerian dishes.

SESAME SEEDS: Toasted sesame seeds are often sprinkled over stews or pastries as a garnish. To toast sesame seeds, see page 24.

TABIL, TAWABIL, OR TABIL KARWYIA: This traditional Tunisian ground-spice blend includes coriander seed, caraway seed, red pepper flakes, and dehydrated garlic. In Tunisia, *tabil* is also the word for caraway seed. (See page 156 for sources in the United States.)

TURMERIC: A ground rhizome used to impart a bright yellow tint to some North African dishes.

SPECIAL EQUIPMENT

COUSCOUSSIER (FRENCH) OR KESKES (ARABIC): The cooking utensil used to make couscous. It is usually made of aluminum, in two parts: The bottom part is a large soup pot used to cook the meat, broth, and vegetables; the top is a tight-fitting colander or sieve in which the couscous is steamed. If you do not have a *couscoussier*, you may substitute a large soup pot topped with a tight-fitting colander. *Couscoussiers* are sometimes available in fine cookware stores and in Middle Eastern markets. Steaming couscous is mandatory for the non-instant variety. Although instant couscous also lends itself to steaming, most users tend to follow the directions on the package, which call for adding hot broth or hot water to the couscous.

MORTAR AND PESTLE: Used to grind spices and dried chilies.

MINT TEA GLASSES: Small, ornately decorated glasses used to serve mint tea. Sometimes found in Middle Eastern or Indian markets.

TAGINE OR TAGINE SLAOUI (PLURAL, TOUAGEN): A Moroccan and Algerian term for the earthenware utensil with a distinctive conical lid in which the stew of the same name traditionally is cooked. (See page 156 for a source for *tagine* dishes in the United States.) The *tagine* (also spelled *tajine*) is traditionally simmered over hot coals. A Dutch oven or a crock pot can be substituted for a *tagine* dish.

BASIC RECIPES

❁

"**S**PICES ARE LIKE WORDS, FULL OF ALCHEMY AND CHARM, AND TRULY BEWITCHING," SAYS WRITER EDMOND AMRAN EL MALEH. LIKE ALCHEMISTS, North African cooks seem to possess an almost innate sense when it comes to seasoning their dishes, performing culinary magic with ground ginger, saffron, a pinch of dried rose petals, a few drops of orange flower water, or a generous amount of the uniquely Tunisian blend of spices called *tabil*. Many of these are available in supermarkets or specialty foods markets, others are found in Middle Eastern markets. (For a list of mail-order sources, see page 156.)

To fully experience the authentic flavors of the cuisine of the Maghreb, I urge you to make two basic condiments: preserved lemons, and aged butter, or *smen*. Both are easy to prepare, but they *must* be made several weeks ahead of time. The fiery Tunisian harissa is also popular throughout North Africa. It is available commercially, but you can just as easily make your own. Although you will be sacrificing some of the true taste of North Africa, you may chose not to use *smen* for dietary reasons. Instead of *smen* you can use Indian *ghee*, available in some Middle Eastern and Indian markets, or substitute equal amounts of butter and olive oil. For sources for preserved lemons, see page 156.

PRESERVED LEMONS THREE WAYS

PRESERVED LEMONS, OR **L'HAMD MRAKAD**, ARE ONE OF THE MOST IMPORTANT SEASONING INGREDIENTS IN MOROCCAN CUISINE. ONCE PRESERVED, THE RIND TURNS TENDER, THE PULP ACQUIRES AN ALMOST JAMLIKE CONSISTENCY, AND THE FLAVOR OF THE LEMON IS INTENSIFIED. THUS PREPARED, PRESERVED LEMONS IMPART THEIR DISTINCTIVE FLAVOR TO A WIDE VARIETY OF DISHES, FROM SAVORY PASTRIES TO STEWS AND SALADS. SINCE THE LEMONS ARE PRESERVED IN SALT, THERE IS USUALLY NO NEED FOR SALTING THE DISH. USUALLY, THE RIND IS CUT UP AND ADDED AT THE END OF THE COOKING PROCESS, AND THE PULP IS BLENDED WITH THE SAUCE. PRESERVED LEMONS ARE ALSO USED TO A LESSER DEGREE IN ALGERIA AND TUNISIA. MOROCCAN COOKS FAVOR THE THIN SKINNED MEYER LEMONS, ALTHOUGH THE THICKER-SKINNED EUREKAS MAY ALSO BE USED.

MOROCCAN-STYLE PRESERVED LEMONS

MAKES 12 LEMONS

Wash and dry the lemons. (If using store-bought lemons, scrub them carefully to remove any pesticides.) Cut a thin slice from the top and the bottom of each lemon. Set one lemon on end and make a vertical cut three quarters of the way through the fruit, so that the two halves still remain attached at the base; do not cut it in half. Turn the lemon upside down and rotate it so that you can make a second vertical cut down the center, crosswise to the first, leaving the bottom attached, as you did previously. Fill each cut with as much salt as it will hold.

Carefully place the lemon at the bottom of a hot, sterilized, wide-mouthed quart glass jar. Proceed in this manner with the remaining lemons, compressing them in the jar until no space is left and the lemon juice has risen to the top. Seal and set aside at room temperature. More lemons may be added in the following days as the lemon rinds begin to soften.

12 unblemished organically grown small lemons, preferably Meyer lemons
Kosher or table salt

Make sure the lemons are covered with juice at all times, adding freshly squeezed lemon juice if necessary. The lemons are ready to use when the rinds are tender, in 5 to 6 weeks. Rinse them lightly before using. Once opened, refrigerate preserved lemons for up to 6 months.

QUICK PRESERVED LEMONS

My friend Peg Rahn is a food writer and the owner of a cooking school in Pasadena, California. When she runs out of preserved lemons, she turns to this quick-preserve method: Cut and fill the lemons with salt as described in the preceding recipe. Place them in a freezer-proof container, seal, and freeze overnight. This causes the lemon rind to soften somewhat. Use in place of traditionally preserved lemons, although the texture of the rind will be tougher and the pulp won't have the jamlike quality of the traditional preserved lemons.

SPICED PRESERVED LEMONS

ALGERIA, TUNISIA

MAKES 8 LEMONS

In Algeria and Tunisia, ground coriander is often added to preserved lemons. Thicker-skinned Eureka lemons are best suited for this recipe. These lemons are less salty than the Moroccan-style preserves.

Scrub the lemons and dry them thoroughly. Cut them into slices ¼-inch thick. Remove the seeds and transfer the slices to a large bowl. Sprinkle with the coriander and 1 tablespoon of the salt. Mix gently. Layer the lemon slices in a hot, sterilized, wide-mouthed quart glass jar, sprinkling each layer with a little salt until all the slices have been added. Add olive oil to cover. Seal tightly and place in a cool, dry place for 2 to 3 weeks. If mold forms on the top, remove it with a clean spoon. Refrigerate after opening, for up to 2 months.

8 unblemished thick-skinned lemons
1 tablespoon ground coriander
2 tablespoons kosher or table salt
1 to 2 cups extra-virgin olive oil

MERYEM'S SMEN

AGED BUTTER (MOROCCO, ALGERIA, TUNISIA)

MAKES 2 CUPS (1 POUND)

FOR WESTERN PALATES, **SMEN** IS DEFINITELY AN ACQUIRED TASTE. FOR NORTH AFRICANS, HOWEVER, THIS PUNGENT AGED BUTTER TREMENDOUSLY ENHANCES THE FLAVOR OF COUSCOUS AND STEWS. AS **SMEN** AGES, IT ACQUIRES A POWERFUL FLAVOR AND AROMA, SOMEWHAT LIKE ROQUEFORT CHEESE, AND THEREFORE SHOULD BE USED SPARINGLY. IT DOESN'T NEED TO BE REFRIGERATED, ALTHOUGH IT SHOULD BE STORED IN A COOL, DRY PLACE. THE MOST HIGHLY PRIZED **SMEN** HAS BEEN AGED FOR SEVERAL YEARS.

2 cups (1 pound) unsalted butter at
    room temperature
½ cup water
1 tablespoon coarse sea salt or kosher salt
¼ cup dried oregano

For me, the word *smen* conjures up memories of my visit with the Kwacem, a tribe of falconers who live two hours south of Casablanca. I had gone there to interview them for an article on falconry. After I had removed my shoes and entered his modest home, Abdallah, the tribal chief, bade me sit on a straw mat on the floor. His wife Meryem brought out a small earthenware pot and set it on a tray in front of us. The pungent aroma of *smen* filled the air as she removed the tightly fitting lid. She placed some *smen* in a bowl before me, along with a colorful woven basket containing freshly baked *kesra* (page 138.) Abdallah, his teenaged daughter, and I spent the better part of the morning savoring warm morsels of *kesra* dipped in the soft *smen,* while sipping glasses of sweet mint tea and discussing the finer points of falconry.

Place the butter in a medium bowl and stir it with a wooden spoon. Set aside. In a small saucepan, boil the water with the salt and oregano until it is reduced to about 6 tablespoons. Strain it through a fine sieve directly onto the butter. With a wooden spoon, blend the mixture thoroughly. Let cool. Some water will settle at the bottom of the bowl.

With your hands, knead the butter until the water is almost completely incorporated. Drain off any excess water. Spoon the butter into a hot, sterilized, wide-mouthed pint glass jar and seal. Store in a cool, dry place for at least 6 weeks before using. Refrigerate after opening.

HARISSA

HOT SAUCE (TUNISIA)

MAKES ABOUT 1/2 CUP

HARISSA HAS BECOME A GENERIC NAME FOR HOT SAUCE THROUGHOUT NORTH AFRICA. HARISSA IS USED AS AN INGREDIENT IN MANY, IF NOT MOST, TUNISIAN DISHES, FROM COUSCOUS (PAGE 108) TO **MECHWYA** (PAGE 63) AND **OJJA** (PAGE 80). IT IS ALSO SERVED AS A DIP FOR CHUNKS OF WARM BREAD. IN TUNISIA, **TABIL** (PAGE 22) ADDS ITS DISTINCTIVE FLAVOR TO HARISSA. MOROCCANS AND ALGERIANS USE GROUND CUMIN INSTEAD OF TABIL. THEY SERVE HARISSA ON THE SIDE, TO BE ADDED TO DISHES ACCORDING TO INDIVIDUAL TASTES. TUNISIANS LIVING IN THE UNITED STATES SUBSTITUTE CHINESE OR THAI CHILI PASTE WHEN THEIR SUPPLY OF HARISSA RUNS SHORT. BOTH CAN BE FOUND IN ASIAN MARKETS. HARISSA IS TRADITIONALLY POUNDED TO A PASTE USING A MORTAR AND PESTLE, BUT A BLENDER WILL WORK JUST AS WELL. BE SURE TO WEAR RUBBER GLOVES WHEN HANDLING THE CHILIES, AND AVOID CONTACT WITH YOUR EYES.

Seed the chilies and cut them up with scissors. Place them in a bowl, cover with warm water, and soak them until they turn quite soft, 15 minutes to 1 hour. Drain them and squeeze out the excess water. Place the chilies in a blender along with the remaining ingredients. Grind to a paste. Place in a small glass jar, cover with a thin layer of olive oil, and seal tightly. Refrigerate for up to 3 or 4 weeks.

NOTE: You can sometimes find small cans or tubes of harissa in specialty markets. For additional sources, see page 156.

6 to 8 *dried New Mexico chilies*

2 *garlic cloves, minced*

½ *teaspoon coarse sea salt*

1 *teaspoon* tabil *(page 22)*

½ *cup extra-virgin olive oil*

BHARAT

ROSE PETAL BLEND (TUNISIA)

MAKES 2 TEASPOONS

THIS INTRIGUING BLEND OF DRIED ROSEBUDS, CINNAMON, AND BLACK PEPPER IS USED TO FLAVOR TUNISIAN COUSCOUS, GROUND MEATS, AND EGG **TAGINES,** OR THE TUNISIAN CRUSTLESS QUICHES. MAKE IT AS YOU NEED IT, SO IT WON'T LOSE ITS FRAGRANCE. DRIED ROSEBUDS (**CHOUCH WARD** IN TUNISIAN) ARE AVAILABLE IN NATURAL FOODS STORES (USUALLY IN THE HERBAL TEA SECTION) AND IN MIDDLE EASTERN MARKETS.

In a spice grinder or with a mortar and pestle, grind all the ingredients to a fine powder.

2 tablespoons dried rosebuds (about 10 buds), stem and calyx removed

½ teaspoon freshly ground black pepper

¼ teaspoon ground cinnamon

KHADIDJA'S TABIL

TUNISIAN SPICE BLEND

MAKES ABOUT 1/2 CUP

TABIL IS TO TUNISIA WHAT CURRY IS TO INDIA. SOMETIMES CALLED **TWABIL** OR **TABIL KARWYA,** TABIL IS A UNIQUELY TUNISIAN BLEND OF SPICES THAT INCLUDES CORIANDER, CARAWAY, RED CHILIES (SIMILAR TO OUR NEW MEXICO RED CHILIES), AND GARLIC. (THE WORD **TABIL** ALSO REFERS TO CARAWAY SEED.) IT SEEMS AS THOUGH EVERY TUNISIAN COOK HAS HIS OR HER OWN VARIATION OF THIS EXTREMELY POPULAR SEASONING. KHADIDJA BOUAZZA, A WIDELY RESPECTED COOK IN HER NEIGHBOR-HOOD OF LA MARSA NEAR TUNIS, IS NO EXCEPTION. SHE USUALLY PREPARES HER TABIL BY THE KILO! I SPENT A FEW HOURS ONE MORNING WATCHING HER ASSEMBLE THE INGREDIENTS NECESSARY FOR HER PARTICULAR BLEND. SHE PAINSTAKINGLY SEEDED A KILO OF DRIED CHILI PODS BEFORE CUTTING THEM UP WITH SCISSORS INTO A LARGE WOODEN BOWL CONTAINING PREMEASURED QUANTITIES OF CORIANDER SEEDS, CARAWAY SEEDS, AND SUN-DRIED, UNPEELED GARLIC CLOVES. "UNPEELED GARLIC ADDS MORE FLAVOR," SHE EXPLAINED, NOTICING MY ASTONISHMENT. SHE TRANSFERRED EVERYTHING TO A WICKER BASKET AND ALLOWED IT TO STAND IN THE SUN UNTIL LATE AFTERNOON, WHEN SHE TOOK IT TO THE NEIGHBORHOOD MILL FOR GRINDING.

¼ cup ground coriander
1 tablespoon ground caraway
1½ tablespoons garlic powder
1 tablespoon New Mexico chili powder
  (see Note)

Mix all the spices and store in an airtight container. Use within 2 months.

NOTE: You will find various chili powders in the Mexican foods section of supermarkets. For additional sources, see page 156.

VEGETABLE BROTH

TAKE THE TIME TO PREPARE THIS FLAVORFUL BROTH. IT WILL ENHANCE THE FLAVOR OF NUMEROUS RECIPES. CANNED VEGETABLE BROTH IS ALSO AVAILABLE COMMERCIALLY.

Stud the onion with the cloves. In a medium saucepan or soup pot, combine all the ingredients except the salt and bring to a boil. Skim off the foam and cover. Reduce the heat and simmer until the broth acquires a full flavor, 1 to 1½ hours. Drain through a fine-meshed sieve into a large bowl. With the back of a spoon, press the vegetables until all the liquid is squeezed out of them. Season with salt. Cover and refrigerate for 2 to 3 days.

1 onion

3 whole cloves

8 cups water

2 small turnips, quartered

2 carrots, peeled and cut into chunks

15 flat leaf parsley sprigs

2 celery stalks or fennel fronds, cut into
　　thirds

15 mushroom stems

10 green onions with tops

2 bay leaves

6 peppercorns

Salt to taste

BASIC TECHNIQUES

TOASTING NUTS: Toasting nuts brings out their flavor. Place the nuts in a dry nonstick skillet over medium-high heat. Shake the pan back and forth, or stir with a wooden spoon until the nuts turn a light brown, 2 or 3 minutes, taking great care not to let them burn (this can happen very quickly!). Remove the nuts from the pan and let cool.

TOASTING SESAME SEEDS: Proceed in the same manner as toasting nuts. Shake the pan back and forth for 1 minute, watching carefully so seeds don't burn. Remove the seeds from pan and let cool.

PEELING AND SEEDING TOMATOES: In a medium saucepan filled with boiling water, blanch the tomatoes for 20 to 30 seconds. Remove them with a slotted spoon and let cool. Remove the peel. To seed, cut the tomatoes in half, hold each half upside down over the sink, and gently squeeze out the seeds.

SOAKING BEANS: Rinse and pick over the beans and soak them overnight in a bowl of water to cover. Drain and proceed with the recipe. For the quick-soak method, place the beans in a large soup pot and add 10 cups of hot water and 2 teaspoons of salt for every pound of dried beans. Bring them to a rolling boil for 2 to 3 minutes. Turn off the heat and let the beans stand in the cooking water for at least 1 hour, and preferably longer. Drain the beans and proceed with the recipe. The older the beans, the longer they will take to cook.

chapter one

APPETIZERS

APPETIZERS

✹

THE HOSPITABLE TREATMENT OF VISITORS IS A TIME-HONORED, ALMOST SACRED, TRADITION THROUGHOUT THE MAGHREB — one undoubtedly nurtured by centuries of nomadic life, during which simple survival was often at stake and solicitude towards all wayfarers was a means of ensuring reciprocal treatment. Today, whether in a modest mountain dwelling or a luxurious city villa, the man of the family is bound by this tradition to honor his guests. Dr. Gerhard Rohlfs, who traveled with the *sherif* (Arab chief) of Ouezzane in northern Morocco in the late 1800s, gives this amusing account of the overwhelming hospitality extended to them by a local *kaid* (district judge) in his book, *Adventures in Morocco and Journeys through the Oases of Draa and Tafilet:*

> These days were regular eating forays, for the more you want to show esteem for a person in Morocco the more food you must set before him. In the evening the *kaid* visited the Grand Sherif in his tent, and was likewise well feasted, but he had hardly departed for the night when he sent us another and yet more plenteous repast, and next morning we had barely finished one substantial breakfast when in came the *kaid* to fetch us to a second, which we could not decline; in short, during our stay here our stomachs had barely an hour's rest.

This generous spirit permeates the culture of the Maghreb. For all its inhabitants, a carefully executed meal served in abundant quantities is the traditional way to honor visitors. In this chapter, I have included several tantalizing appetizers that might be served to guests in a North African home.

DANIELLE'S SUN-DRIED PEPPERS

(MOROCCO, ALGERIA)

MAKES 1 QUART

THESE SWEET PEPPERS ARE COMMONLY SERVED AS AN APPETIZER IN MOROCCO AND ALGERIA. DANIELLE MAMANE, A FRIEND OF MINE WHO LIVES IN THE ANCIENT CITY OF FEZ, THE CULINARY CAPITAL OF MOROCCO, TAUGHT ME HOW TO MAKE THEM. IN SUMMER, AT THE HEIGHT OF THE SEASON, DANIELLE DRIES HUNDREDS OF RED BELL PEPPERS ON THE FLAT TILED ROOF OF HER HOME. AFTER THEY ARE PRESERVED IN OLIVE OIL, SHE WILL HAVE A SUPPLY THAT WILL LAST THROUGHOUT THE YEAR. ALTHOUGH THEY ARE USUALLY SERVED AS AN APPETIZER, I FIND THAT THESE PEPPERS MAKE A FINE TOPPING FOR PIZZA, JUST LIKE SUN-DRIED TOMATOES, THE FLAVOR OF THE PEPPERS IS INTENSIFIED BY THE DRYING PROCESS. MARINATE THEM FOR AT LEAST 2 WEEKS BEFORE USING.

10 pounds (about 20) red bell peppers
Extra-virgin olive oil to cover

Over an open flame or under a preheated broiler, grill the peppers, turning them carefully with tongs, until the skins are evenly blackened. Transfer them to paper or plastic bags and close them. When the peppers are cool enough to handle, peel and seed them. Pat them dry with paper towels and cut them into ½-inch-thick strips. Line several baking sheets with clean towels or paper towels. Place the pepper strips on top and place the baking sheets outdoors in full sun. Cover with cheesecloth. Sun-dry the peppers until they acquire the same consistency as soft leather, much like sun-dried tomatoes. This may take more than 1 day; if so, bring the peppers in at night. To preserve the peppers, place them in a hot, steril-ized, wide-mouthed 1-quart jar and cover with olive oil. Seal and refrigerate for 1 to 2 weeks. Bring the peppers to room temperature before serving. The peppers will keep for up to 6 months in the refrigerator.

CHEESE MANTECAOS

CHEESE PUFFS (ALGERIA, MOROCCO)

MAKES ABOUT 35 MANTECAOS

SEPHARDIC COOKS IN ALGERIA AND MOROCCO OFTEN SERVE THESE SAVORY CHEESE PUFFS AS PART OF AN ARRAY OF TASTY APPETIZERS CALLED **KEMIA.** SIMILAR TO THE TAPAS SERVED IN SPAIN, **KEMIA** OFTEN INCLUDE BOWLS OF PICKLED VEGETABLES OR GRILLED ALMONDS SPRINKLED WITH CUMIN, AS WELL AS THESE **MANTECAOS.** WHEN THEY COME OUT OF THE OVEN, **MANTECAOS** TAKE ON THE TEXTURE AND APPEARANCE OF SMALL MACAROONS.

¾ cup (1½ sticks) unsalted butter, at
    room temperature
2 cups coarsely grated (8 ounces) Swiss
    or Gruyère cheese
1½ cups unbleached all-purpose flour
1 egg yolk
½ teaspoon salt
¼ teaspoon cayenne
2 teaspoons cumin seeds
Sweet paprika for garnish (optional)

Preheat the oven to 450°F. In a large bowl, blend together all the ingredients except the paprika. Separate the mixture into 2 equal parts. In a food processor, mix each half by briefly pulsing on and off 8 to 10 times, or until the ingredients are coarsely blended. Or, with a pastry blender or 2 knives, mix the dough until it acquires the consistency of coarse crumbs. Do not let the mixture turn into a homogeneous dough.

Using 1 tablespoon of dough at a time, roll into balls about 1 inch in diameter. Place the balls on a nonstick or an aluminum foil–lined baking sheet and flatten them slightly with your fingers. Place the pan on the middle shelf of the oven and bake the pastries until they puff slightly and turn golden, 10 to 12 minutes. Let them cool completely on a wire rack. With a spatula, transfer them to a serving platter. Sprinkle with paprika, if using.

SFERYA WITH BESSARA

CHEESE BALLS WITH GARBANZO BEAN DIP (ALGERIA)

MAKES ABOUT 50 SFERYA

SFERYA ARE THE LITTLE CHEESE BALLS FREQUENTLY USED TO RING A PLATTER HOLDING AN ALGERIAN **TAGINE.** THE INTRIGUING MIXTURE INCLUDES BREAD CRUMBS, A CHEESE SIMILAR TO GREEK FETA, AND ORANGE FLOWER WATER. MY ADAPTATION OF **SFERYA** IS SERVED AS AN APPETIZER WITH **BESSARA,** A SPICED PUREE OF GARBANZO BEANS.

SFERYA

2 cups dried bread crumbs

4 eggs, lightly beaten

4 ounces Greek feta cheese, crumbled
   (about 1 cup)

2 tablespoons orange flower water
   (page 12)

½ teaspoon baking powder

½ teaspoon ground cinnamon

6 fresh flat-leaf parsley sprigs, minced

2 tablespoons grated or minced onion

2 tablespoons vegetable oil

Vegetable oil for deep-frying

To make the *sferya:* Preheat the oven to 200°F. In large bowl, mix all the ingredients until you obtain a fairly smooth dough. Using about 2 teaspoons of dough, roll into ¾-inch-diameter balls. In a heavy medium pot, pour vegetable oil to a depth of 2 inches. Heat over medium-high heat to 325°F, or until a piece of the dough sizzles instantly. Drop 5 or 6 balls at a time into the hot oil and fry, turning with tongs, until golden brown, about 3 or 4 minutes. Drain well on paper towels. Place on a baking sheet and keep warm in the oven. Repeat until all the balls are fried.

BESSARA

½ cup canned garbanzo beans, drained
   and liquid reserved

1 tablespoon fresh lemon juice

½ teaspoon ground cumin

1 garlic clove, minced

¼ teaspoon sweet paprika

To make the bessara: In a blender or food processor, puree the garbanzo beans with ⅓ cup of their liquid until smooth. Transfer to a small bowl and mix with the lemon juice, cumin, and garlic. Sprinkle with the paprika. Serve the warm *sferya* with toothpicks and with the *bessara* alongside.

DOIGTS DE FATMA

FATIMA'S FINGERS (TUNISIA, ALGERIA)

MAKES 12 TO 14 FINGERS

THESE DELICACIES, CALLED **DOIGTS DE FATMA** IN TUNISIA (FATIMA WAS THE DAUGHTER OF THE PROPHET MOHAMMED), AND **DOIGTS DE LA MARIÉE** (BRIDE'S FINGERS) IN ALGERIA, ARE SIMILAR TO MOROCCAN **BRIOUATS.** THEY ARE THE NORTH AFRICAN COUNTERPART TO CHINESE EGG ROLLS AND MAY BE EITHER BAKED OR FRIED. INDEED, EGG ROLL SKINS ARE USED HERE AS A GOOD SUBSTITUTE FOR TUNISIAN **MALSOUKA,** THE DOUGH TRADITIONALLY USED TO MAKE DOIGTS DE FATMA.

Traditional cooks prefer the frying method, which yields a crispier pastry. Baking is a common alternative, however, although the dough must be brushed with butter before filling. Unlike the Moroccan version, which resemble small plump cigars, these fingers are long and slender and are sometimes open at one end.

In a medium skillet over medium-high heat, heat the oil and cook the potatoes and onion, stirring occasionally, until the potatoes are tender, 20 to 25 minutes. Stir in the garlic and cook a few minutes longer. If the mixture becomes too dry, add 1 or 2 tablespoons of water. Transfer to a medium bowl and mash the potatoes lightly with a fork. Add the lemon rind, parsley, green onions, paprika, harissa, and salt (remember that preserved lemons already contain salt). Set aside to cool.

To bake the fingers, preheat the oven to 425°F. Separate the egg roll skins carefully and place them on a damp towel. Brush each skin with melted butter. Place 1 heaping tablespoon of filling at the base of each skin. Fold over the sides and roll up. Repeat the process until all the filling is used. Place the fingers on a nonstick or a lightly greased baking sheet and bake until golden brown, 15 to 20 minutes. Drain well on paper towels. Serve hot at once with the lemon wedges.

To fry the fingers, in a medium saucepan, pour oil to a depth of 2 inches. Heat over medium-high heat until the oil reaches 325°F, or a piece of the dough sizzles instantly. Fry the pastries in batches to avoid crowding them until golden, about 6 to 8 minutes, and drain them well on paper towels. Serve as directed above.

NOTE: To freeze, place single layers of uncooked fingers in a freeze-proof container, separating them with sheets of waxed paper or plastic wrap. It isn't necessary to thaw the fingers, but cook them for an additional 3 or 4 minutes.

2 tablespoons olive oil

3 boiling potatoes (about 1 pound), peeled and cut into ¼-inch cubes

1 large onion, finely diced

1 or 2 tablespoons water (optional)

6 garlic cloves, minced

2 teaspoons finely chopped preserved lemon rind (page 15)

¼ cup minced fresh flat-leaf parsley

3 green onions with tops, finely sliced

½ teaspoon sweet paprika

Harissa to taste (page 19)

Salt to taste

Fourteen 7-inch-square Chinese egg roll skins

Vegetable oil for frying (optional)

Lemon wedges for garnish

GARLIC AND CHEESE BETZELS

PHYLLO TRIANGLES (ALGERIA)

MAKES 32 BETZELS

BETZELS, OR **PASTELS**, IS THE SEPHARDIC TERM FOR WHAT THE ALGERIANS CALL **SAMSAS** AND THE MOROCCANS CALL **BRIOUATS**. WHETHER ROLLED INTO THE SHAPE OF A CIGAR OR SHAPED INTO TASTY LITTLE TRIANGLES, **BETZELS** CAN ENFOLD A VARIETY OF FILLINGS, FROM CHEESE TO MEATS AND SEAFOOD. THESE PARTICULAR **BETZELS** CANNOT BE FROZEN, BUT THEY WILL KEEP UNCOOKED IN AN AIR-TIGHT CONTAINER IN THE REFRIGERATOR FOR 3 OR 4 DAYS.

In a medium saucepan, place 6 of the eggs, add water to cover, and bring the water to a low boil. Cook the eggs for 12 to 15 minutes. Drain and let cool. Peel, place the eggs in a medium bowl, and mash them coarsely with a fork. Mix in the cheese, garlic, parsley, mint, olives, salt, pepper, paprika, and 1 lightly beaten raw egg.

Cover a working surface with a damp towel. Carefully unwrap the phyllo and unfold it on the towel. With the long edge of the phyllo facing you, and using a sharp knife, cut vertically through the stacked sheets of dough to make 4 equal sections, each about 4½ inches wide. Cover with another damp towel if you are not using the phyllo immediately.

Place 1 tablespoon of the filling about 1 inch from the bottom edge of one strip. Fold over a bottom corner of the strip to cover the filling. Continue folding as you would a flag, to obtain a triangular shape. Beat the remaining egg and use it to seal the top edge. Repeat the process until all the filling has been used.

In a heavy, medium saucepan, pour oil to a depth of 2 inches and heat it over medium-high heat until it reaches 325°F, or a piece of the dough sizzles instantly. Fry the pastries in batches to avoid crowding them, until golden, about 6 to 8 minutes, and drain them well on paper towels. Serve at once with lemon wedges.

8 eggs

1 cup (4 ounces) freshly grated Gruyère cheese

10 to 12 garlic cloves, minced

24 fresh flat-leaf parsley sprigs, minced

5 fresh mint leaves, minced

12 green olives, pitted and minced

Salt and freshly ground black pepper to taste

2 teaspoons sweet paprika

8 sheets (about 8 ounces) frozen phyllo dough, thawed

Vegetable oil for frying

Lemon wedges for garnish

SPINACH BRIOUATS

SPINACH PHYLLO CIGARS (MOROCCO)

MAKES ABOUT 60 **BRIOUATS**

BRIOUATS (PRONOUNCED "BRĒWǍTS") ARE CIGAR-SHAPED PHYLLO PASTRIES WITH A VARIETY OF SWEET OR SAVORY FILLINGS. THEY ARE SERVED AS APPETIZERS OR AS A FIRST COURSE. **BRIOUATS** ARE TRADITIONALLY FRIED, ALTHOUGH THEY ARE SOMETIMES BAKED. FRYING YIELDS A SLIGHTLY CRISPIER PASTRY. IF YOU PLAN TO BAKE THEM, THE PHYLLO MUST BE BRUSHED WITH MELTED BUTTER BEFORE FILLING. THIS ISN'T NECESSARY WHEN DEEP-FRYING, HOWEVER.

Two 10-ounce packages frozen chopped spinach, cooked and drained

4 ounces fresh white goat or Greek feta cheese, crumbled (about 1 cup)

2 eggs, lightly beaten

1 cup dried bread crumbs

20 fresh flat-leaf parsley sprigs, minced

8 fresh mint leaves, minced

2 garlic cloves, minced

1 small onion, finely chopped

Salt and freshly ground black pepper to taste

15 sheets (about 1 pound) thawed frozen phyllo dough

¾ cup (1½ sticks) butter, melted (optional)

Vegetable oil for frying (optional)

Lemon wedges for garnish

Squeeze as much liquid as you can from the spinach. In a medium bowl, mix the spinach with the cheese, eggs, bread crumbs, parsley, mint, garlic, onion, salt, and pepper. Set aside.

Cover a work surface with a damp towel. Carefully unwrap the phyllo and unfold it on the towel. With the long edge of the phyllo facing you, and using a sharp knife, cut vertically through the stacked sheets of dough to make 4 equal sections, each about 4½ inches wide. If you plan to bake the cigars, preheat the oven to 425°F and brush the dough with melted butter.

Place 1 heaping teaspoon of filling at the base of each strip. Fold over the sides and roll up. Repeat the process until all the filling has been used. Any remaining phyllo can be rewrapped and refrigerated. The *briouats* are now ready for frying, baking, or freezing (see Note).

To fry, in a heavy, medium saucepan, pour oil to a depth of 2 inches and heat it over medium-high heat until it reaches 325°F, or a piece of the dough sizzles instantly. Fry the pastries in batches to avoid crowding them, until golden, about 6 to 8 minutes, and drain them well on paper towels. Serve at once with lemon wedges.

To bake, place the *briouats* on a nonstick or aluminum foil–lined baking sheet. Bake until golden brown, 12 to 15 minutes. Serve at once with lemon wedges.

NOTE: To freeze uncooked *briouats,* place them in a single layer on a baking sheet so they freeze individually. Transfer them to an airtight container, separating them with waxed paper or plastic wrap. They will keep for up to 2 months. Do not thaw the *briouats* before frying or baking.

MECHWYA CANAPÉS

(TUNISIA)

MAKES ABOUT 24 CANAPÉS

THESE FLAVORFUL HORS D'OEUVRES ARE MADE WITH THE TUNISIAN PEPPER SALAD CALLED **MECHWYA.** YOU WILL NEED ABOUT HALF A RECIPE FOR THIS AMOUNT OF CANAPÉS.

1 fresh baguette

Harissa to taste (page 19)

4 ounces fresh white goat cheese at room temperature

2 cups mechwya (page 63)

2 hard-cooked eggs, chopped

Cut the baguette into ½-inch-thick slices. Lightly paint each slice with harissa. Spread with goat cheese. Spoon some *mechwya* on each slice. Press the eggs through a medium-meshed sieve and sprinkle a little on each slice.

chapter two

SOUPS AND
SALADS

SOUPS AND SALADS

SOUPS

FOR ME, MAKING A WONDERFULLY NUTRITIOUS SOUP LIKE **HARIRA** (PAGE 41) OR **CHORBA** (PAGE 48), IS ONE OF THE MOST DELICIOUS WAYS TO BRING BACK MEMORIES OF MY CHILDHOOD. Throughout the day, as exotic smells waft through the house, I am mentally transported back to the kitchens of my mother and grandmother, where a vegetable-based soup was daily fare.

Many traditional Moroccan, Algerian, and Tunisian soups forego the use of meat, relying instead on less-expensive legumes, such as dried fava beans, garbanzo beans, and lentils, as sources of protein. Fava beans, among the world's oldest and most widely used legumes, were already a staple of the Maghreb's indigenous Berbers when Phoenician traders first set foot on North African soil.

In Tunisia, a vegetable soup filled with a small spindle-shaped pasta called *hlelem* (page 42) often begins the meal. There, as in the rest of North Africa, hearty vegetable chorbas, thickened with egg noodles, often serve as the entree for a supper *en famille.*

Most of the soups in this chapter can be served as a main course, accompanied only with a tossed green salad and a crusty loaf of fresh bread. The recipes that call for beans can be made with dried or canned beans. You will find a recipe for vegetable broth on page 23, should you want to make your own. The canned vegetable broth sold in supermarkets serves as a convenient substitute.

HARIRA

LENTIL AND GARBANZO BEAN SOUP (MOROCCO)

SERVES 8

HARIRA IS THE HEARTY BEAN SOUP, REDOLENT OF CINNAMON AND GINGER, WITH WHICH MOROCCAN FAMILIES TRADITIONALLY BREAK THE DAY'S FAST EACH EVENING DURING THE MOSLEM MONTH OF RAMADAN, THE NINTH AND HOLIEST MONTH OF THE MOSLEM LUNAR CALENDAR, WHICH COMMEMORATES THE FIRST REVELATION OF THE KORAN. AT SUNSET, ALL SIGNS OF LIFE DISAPPEAR FROM THE CITY STREETS. EVERYONE IS AT HOME ENJOYING A STEAMING BOWL OF **HARIRA**, A FEW DATES, AND A GLASS OF MILK. IN THE COUNTRYSIDE, MANY MOROCCAN FARMERS OFTEN START THEIR DAY WITH A BOWL OF **HARIRA**.

In a soup pot over medium-high heat, heat the oil and cook the onions, stirring occasionally, until tender, 6 to 8 minutes. In a blender or food processor, combine the tomatoes, ginger, cinnamon, turmeric, saffron, cilantro, parsley, salt, and pepper. Puree the mixture, in batches if necessary, until fairly smooth. Add to the onions and bring to a boil. Add the lentils and water. Cover tightly and reduce heat to low. Simmer the soup until the lentils are tender, 30 to 35 minutes. Add the undrained garbanzo beans and the *foul mudammas* and bring the soup back to a low boil. Add the pasta and cook until tender, 6 to 8 minutes. Add the egg and stir until it forms strands in the soup. Ladle the soup into bowls and serve with lemon wedges.

NOTE: Canned fava beans, called *foul mudammas,* are available in Middle Eastern and Italian markets, and sometimes in the specialty section of large supermarkets. Dried fava beans and dried garbanzo beans are also available. To cook dried beans, follow the quick-soak method on page 24. Drain the beans, and cook them, covered, over low heat, until they are tender, 3 to 4 hours. Drain again and proceed with the recipe. The older the bean, the longer the cooking time.

2 tablespoons olive oil

2 onions, sliced

One 28-ounce can whole tomatoes

¼ teaspoon ground ginger

¼ teaspoon ground cinnamon

¼ teaspoon ground turmeric

8 Spanish saffron threads, crushed

20 fresh cilantro sprigs

10 fresh flat-leaf parsley sprigs

Salt and freshly ground black pepper to taste

1 cup lentils, rinsed and picked over

8 cups water

One 15-ounce can garbanzo beans with their liquid

One 15-ounce can foul mudammas with their liquid (see Note)

½ cup broken dried thin egg noodles or capellini (angel hair) pasta (about 2 ½ ounces)

1 egg, lightly beaten

Lemon wedges for garnish

HLELEM

BEAN, CHARD, AND NOODLE SOUP (TUNISIA)

SERVES 4

THIS HEARTY SOUP IS SERVED YEAR-ROUND IN TUNISIA, OFTEN AS A MAIN COURSE FOR LUNCH OR DINNER. **HLELEM** IS THE NAME GIVEN TO THE HAND-ROLLED PASTA AS WELL AS TO THE SOUP IN WHICH IT IS USED. MEHERZIA JAZIRI, A FRIEND WHO RESIDES IN GAMMARTH, A HISTORIC SEASIDE RESORT NORTH OF TUNIS, INSISTS ON MAKING HER OWN PASTA, EVEN THOUGH IT IS AVAILABLE AT HER LOCAL MARKET. "IT'S JUST NOT AS GOOD AS HOMEMADE," SHE DECLARES, AS SHE PATIENTLY ROLLS TINY PELLETS OF DOUGH BETWEEN HER FINGERS TO FORM SHORT, THIN PIECES OF PASTA.

2 tablespoons olive oil

1 small onion, finely diced

½ cup chopped celery leaves

4 cups vegetable broth (page 23)

One 6-ounce can tomato paste

One 15-ounce can butter beans with
their liquid

One 15-ounce can garbanzo beans with
their liquid

1 pound Swiss chard, stems included,
finely chopped

20 fresh flat-leaf parsley sprigs, minced

½ cup crushed dried capellini (angel
hair) pasta or thin egg noodles

Salt and freshly ground black pepper
to taste

2 teaspoons harissa (page 19)

Lemon wedges for garnish

In this recipe, I substitute either threadlike capellini or thin egg noodles, breaking them up before adding them to the soup. I also use canned garbanzo beans as well as canned butter beans (sometimes called large lima beans). If you prefer to use dried beans, however, follow the quick-soak method (page 24). You can also make *hlelem* with small navy beans or lentils.

In a large saucepan or soup pot over medium-high heat, heat the oil and cook the onion, stirring occasionally, until tender, 6 to 8 minutes. Add the celery leaves and stir until wilted. Add the broth and the tomato paste and stir to blend. Bring to a low boil. Add the butter beans, garbanzo beans, chard, parsley, and crushed pasta or noodles. Cook, covered, until the vegetables are tender, 10 to 15 minutes. Season with salt, pepper, and harissa. Serve with lemon wedges on the side.

NOTE: Canned butter beans and canned garbanzo beans are available in most supermarkets. Dried varieties are also available. Drain the beans, and cook them, covered, over low heat, until they are tender, 3 to 4 hours. Drain and proceed with the recipe. The older the bean, the longer the cooking time.

THREE-BEAN BERKOUKSH

BEAN AND PASTINI SOUP (ALGERIA)

SERVES 4 TO 6

BERKOUKSH IS AN ALGERIAN SOUP SIMILAR TO MINESTRONE. IT GETS ITS NAME FROM THE SMALL PASTA PELLETS USED TO THICKEN IT. THE ITALIANS CALL THESE **PASTINI** OR **ACINI DI PEPE** (LITTLE PEPPERCORNS). THE PIEDS-NOIRS KNOW THEM AS **PETITS PLOMBS,** OR LEAD PELLETS. CILANTRO AND MINT ADD A LIGHT, REFRESHING TOUCH TO THIS **BERKOUKSH.**

Soak and drain the lima and fava beans (see page 24). Set aside. In a soup pot or a small Dutch oven over medium-high heat, heat the oil and cook the onions, stirring occasionally, until tender, 6 to 8 minutes. Add the tomatoes, paprika, turmeric, garlic, and 12 of the cilantro sprigs tied with cotton string. Bring to a boil and add the broth or water, carrot, and optional jalapeño. Reduce the heat to medium, cover, and cook until the carrot is crisp-tender, 8 to 10 minutes. Add the drained soaked lima and fava beans. Reduce the heat to medium low, cover, and cook until the beans are tender, 3 to 4 hours.

Fifteen minutes before serving, discard the cilantro and turn the heat to medium-high. Add the frozen baby lima beans and the pasta and cook until tender, 8 to 10 minutes. Season with salt and pepper. Chop the remaining 12 cilantro sprigs and the fresh mint, and stir into the soup. Transfer the *berkouksh* to a tureen. Add the *smen*, if using. Serve with lemon wedges.

1 cup each large dried lima beans and dried fava beans

2 tablespoons olive oil

2 large onions, finely diced

One 28-ounce can crushed tomatoes in puree

1 tablespoon sweet paprika

1 teaspoon ground turmeric

4 garlic cloves, minced

24 fresh cilantro sprigs

7 cups vegetable broth (page 23) or water

1 large carrot, peeled and cut into ½-inch slices

1 jalapeño chili, seeded and minced (optional)

One 10-ounce package frozen baby lima beans

½ cup pastini or acini di pepe pasta

Salt and freshly ground black pepper to taste

10 fresh mint sprigs, minced

1 tablespoon smen (page 18), (optional)

Lemon wedges for garnish

SOUPE AUX POIS CHICHES ET AU POTIRON

GARBANZO BEAN AND PUMPKIN SOUP (MOROCCO)

SERVES 4

CRESCENT-SHAPED SECTIONS OF MEDITERRANEAN SQUASH ADD THEIR FESTIVE ORANGE COLOR TO VEGETABLE STANDS IN MARKETS ALL OVER NORTH AFRICA. THIS DELICIOUS VEGETABLE IS USED IN A WIDE VARIETY OF DISHES, FROM SOUPS TO COUSCOUS. BECAUSE MEDITERRANEAN SQUASH ISN'T COMMONLY AVAILABLE IN THIS COUNTRY, OTHER VARIETIES LIKE BUTTERNUT, ACORN SQUASH, OR SUGAR PUMPKIN MAY BE SUBSTITUTED. FOR A THINNER SOUP, ADD A LITTLE MORE BROTH, WATER, OR MILK.

Preheat the oven to 375°F. Place the squash in an ovenproof dish and cover it tightly with aluminum foil. Bake until tender, 50 minutes to 1 hour. Let cool, then peel and seed the squash and scoop the pulp from the shell. Set the pulp aside.

Meanwhile, in a large saucepan over medium-high heat, heat the oil and cook the onion, stirring occasionally, until tender, 6 to 8 minutes. Let cool.

In a blender or food processor, puree, in batches if necessary, the squash, onion, broth, reserved liquid from the garbanzo beans, and half of the garbanzo beans. Return the puree to the pan. Stir in the tomato paste, salt, pepper, and cayenne. Heat the soup through and add the remaining whole garbanzo beans. Before serving, sprinkle with the minced cilantro.

1 pound Mediterranean, butternut, or acorn squash, or sugar pumpkin

2 tablespoons vegetable oil

1 large onion, finely diced

3 cups vegetable broth (page 23)

One 15-ounce can garbanzo beans, liquid drained and reserved

2 tablespoons tomato paste

Salt and freshly ground black pepper to taste

⅛ teaspoon cayenne

12 fresh cilantro sprigs, minced

LOUBIA B'DERSA

ALGERIAN CHILI

SERVES 6 TO 8

LOUBIA, AN ALGERIAN SPECIALTY, GETS ITS FLAVOR FROM **DERSA**, A SPICY BLEND OF GROUND RED CHILIES, GARLIC, AND GROUND CUMIN. DERSA IS A PREDOMINANT SEASONING IN MANY ALGERIAN DISHES. A DASH OF VINEGAR IS TRADITIONALLY ADDED TO EACH BOWL OF LOUBIA ON SERVING.

1 pound (2 cups) small dried navy
   beans

¼ cup olive oil

1 large onion, finely diced

3 small dried red chilies, seeded

15 garlic cloves, minced

1 tablespoon sweet paprika

¼ teaspoon freshly ground black pepper

4 teaspoons ground cumin

One 6-ounce can tomato paste

2 tomatoes, coarsely chopped

7 cups water or vegetable broth
   (see page 23)

2 bay leaves

⅛ teaspoon cayenne

20 fresh flat-leaf parsley sprigs, minced

2½ teaspoons salt

10 fresh cilantro sprigs, chopped

Cider vinegar or red wine vinegar
   (optional)

Soak and drain the beans (see page 24). Set aside. In a large soup pot over medium-high heat, heat the oil, and cook the onion, stirring occasionally, until tender, 6 to 8 minutes. Add the chilies, garlic, paprika, pepper, and cumin. Cook, stirring, for 2 to 3 minutes. Add the tomato paste and cook, stirring, until the mixture thickens, 1 to 2 minutes. Stir in the tomatoes and 1 cup of the water or broth and bring to a boil. Add the beans, the remaining 6 cups water or broth, the bay leaves, cayenne, and 10 of the parsley sprigs tied together with cotton string. Mince the remaining parsley and set aside. Lower the heat to medium low, cover, and cook the beans until tender, 1 to 2 hours.

Before serving, discard the chilies, bay leaves, and tied parsley. Season with salt. Stir in the reserved minced parsley and cilantro. Serve hot with vinegar on the side, if you like.

SOUPE DE FÈVES

FRESH FAVA BEAN SOUP (ALGERIA)

SERVES 6

MY GREAT-GRANDMOTHER, A SPRY NONAGENARIAN, WAS KNOWN TO THE FAMILY AS MAMAN DARMON. BECAUSE OF HER HIGH ENERGY AND THE SPEED WITH WHICH SHE WHIRLED AROUND THE KITCHEN, WE SOMETIMES CALLED HER **PETIT TAXI**, AFTER THE SMALL RED AND BLACK CABS THAT DARTED IN AND OUT OF THE FEARSOME CASABLANCA TRAFFIC. DURING PASSOVER CELEBRATIONS, IT WASN'T UNUSUAL TO FIND HER IN THE THROES OF HER ANNUAL SPRING CLEANING, PERCHED PRECARIOUSLY ON A LADDER, CHASING COBWEBS FROM THE CORNERS OF HER TWELVE-FOOT CEILINGS. WHEN THAT WAS DONE TO HER SATISFACTION, SHE WOULD DIRECT THE PREPARATION OF TRADITIONAL DISHES LIKE THIS DELICIOUS FRESH FAVA BEAN SOUP.

In a large saucepan or soup pot, combine the fava or lima beans, turnips, carrot, celery, onion, potatoes, bay leaves, and water. Cover and cook until the vegetables are tender, 15 to 20 minutes. Remove the pan from the heat and let cool.

Discard the bay leaves. In a blender or food processor, puree the vegetables and their broth, in batches if necessary, until smooth. Return the mixture to the pan. Season with cumin, salt, and pepper and heat through. Add the cilantro, reserving a few leaves for garnish. Serve with harissa on the side, if you like, and garnish with cilantro.

2 pounds fresh fava beans, shelled and
  peeled, or one 16-ounce package
  frozen baby lima beans

2 turnips, peeled and quartered

1 carrot, peeled and cut into 1-inch
  pieces

2 celery stalks, cut into 1-inch pieces

1 small onion, diced

2 small potatoes, peeled and diced

2 bay leaves

6 cups water

1½ teaspoons ground cumin

Salt and freshly ground black pepper
  to taste

40 fresh cilantro sprigs, stemmed

Harissa (page 19), (optional)

CHORBA EL KHODRA

VEGETABLE SOUP (TUNISIA)

SERVES 6 TO 8

THIS **CHORBA EL KHODRA** (PRONOUNCED "HŌDRĂ") IS THICKENED WITH A SMALL RICE-LIKE PASTA CALLED **CHORBA**, SIMILAR TO ITALIAN ORZO. THE VEGETABLES SHOULD BE CUT INTO CUBES OF UNIFORM SIZE, AND THE CABBAGE FINELY SHREDDED. **TABIL**, A UNIQUELY TUNISIAN BLEND OF SPICES, GIVES THIS SOUP ITS DISTINCTIVE FLAVOR. YOU CAN USE ANY TYPE OF WINTER SQUASH OR PUMPKIN FOR THIS SOUP.

2 tablespoons olive oil

1 large onion, finely diced

3 garlic cloves, minced

2 carrots, peeled and diced

4 celery stalks, cut into ¼-inch dice

2 large tomatoes, peeled and cubed

1 boiling potato (about 6 ounces),
  peeled and cut into ¼-inch dice

7 cups water or vegetable broth
  (page 23)

One 15-ounce can crushed tomatoes

3 tablespoons tomato paste

8 fresh basil leaves, shredded

10 fresh flat-leaf parsley sprigs, minced

2 teaspoons harissa (page 19)

8 ounces winter squash, peeled and cut
  into ½-inch dice

½ small cabbage (about 8 ounces),
  shredded

2 tablespoons tabil *(page 22)*

Salt to taste

¼ cup orzo

Lemon wedges for garnish

In a large soup pot over medium-high heat, heat the oil and cook the onion and the garlic, stirring occasionally, until tender, 6 to 8 minutes. Add the carrots and cook, stirring, until lightly browned, 2 to 3 minutes. Add the celery, fresh tomatoes, potato, water or broth, canned tomatoes, tomato paste, basil, parsley, and harissa. Cover and bring to a low boil. Cook until the potato is tender, 15 to 20 minutes.

Reduce the heat to medium and add the squash and the cabbage. Cover and cook until they are tender, 10 to 15 minutes. Add the tabil, salt, and orzo. Cook until the orzo is tender, 8 to 10 minutes. Serve hot, with lemon wedges and extra harissa on the side.

CHORBA BIL MATISHA

TOMATO SOUP WITH THIN EGG NOODLES (MOROCCO, ALGERIA, TUNISIA)

SERVES 4

CHORBA IS THE SOUPE DU JOUR IN MANY HOUSEHOLDS THROUGHOUT NORTH AFRICA. THIS FLAVORFUL DISH IS MADE WITH VEGETABLE BROTH, PUREED FRESH VEGETABLES, AND BITS OF PASTA.

1 onion

4 whole cloves

6 cups vegetable broth (page 23)

2 pounds butternut squash, peeled, seeded, and cut into small chunks

4 celery stalks, including leaves, coarsely chopped

5 tomatoes (about 2 pounds), quartered

12 fresh cilantro sprigs, tied with cotton string

¼ teaspoon ground turmeric

¼ cup broken dried thin egg noodles or capellini (angel hair) pasta

1 cup milk

Salt and freshly ground black pepper to taste

Lemon wedges for garnish

Stud the onion with the cloves. In a large saucepan or a soup pot, combine the broth, squash, celery, tomatoes, cilantro, and turmeric. Cover and bring to a boil. Reduce heat to medium and cook until the vegetables are tender, 30 to 40 minutes. Discard the onion, cloves, and cilantro. Cool a few minutes.

In a blender, food processor, or ricer, puree the vegetables and the broth, in batches if necessary, to obtain a smooth, thick puree. Return the soup to the pot. Add the pasta and simmer until tender, 6 to 8 minutes. Thin with milk and heat through. Season with salt and pepper. Serve immediately, with lemon wedges.

SALADS

AMONG THE MEMORIES I MOST CHERISH OF MY GIRLHOOD IN CASABLANCA IS THAT OF ACCOMPANY-ING MY MOTHER AND GRANDMOTHER TO THE BEAUTIFUL **MARCHÉ CENTRAL**, the city's bustling central market. Here, they purchased each day the ingredients for some of the delightful salads that I have included in this chapter.

Early in the morning the market was always a beehive of activity. Farmers had arrived before dawn from the fertile Chaouia plain, the agricultural region just outside the city, to ensure that their freshly picked produce would arrive in time for the earliest shoppers.

To get to market, these family farmers employed every means of conveyance available: horsedrawn wagons and rickety donkey carts that sagged under the weight of fresh fruits and vegetables; loud, sputtering mopeds filled with enormous wicker baskets that overflowed with bunches of parsley and cilantro; and, for the more affluent, small trucks so overloaded that they often left a trail of potatoes, carrots, or turnips on the road behind them.

At the entrance to the market, we'd be greeted by Hassan, the mint seller, seated on a wicker mat behind mountains of the fragrant herb. He would always welcome me with a sprig, which I would crush between the palms of my hands in order to inhale the refreshing scent. While my mother and grandmother completed their purchases, I made my way around the market, greeted by vendors who tempted me with a honey-sweet date here, or a few roasted almonds there. *"Mademoiselle! Regarde comme c'est frais!"* ("Miss, look how fresh this is!") exclaimed the fruit vendor, enticing me with a slice of sweet and juicy watermelon. Then as now, bargaining was de rigueur, and I loved to listen to the good-natured haggling that went on as housewives, under the watchful eye of the merchant, tested the firmness of a shiny globe of bright purple eggplant, carefully inspected an emerald green pepper, or selected, one by one, a kilo of crimson tomatoes.

Unlike American markets, where the jet age makes available on a year-round basis almost every type of produce, the fruits and vegetables at the Casablanca market changed with the seasons. The salads served in the Maghreb reflect not only the seasonal variety of produce, but also the creativity of the cook. For in this region of the Mediterranean, the word *salad* means far more than a few leaves of lettuce tossed with some dressing. It refers to the exotically seasoned dishes of either cooked or raw vegetables that are served at the beginning of the meal—usually in a small fleet of bowls, each filled with a different delicious creation. Winter was the season for the fresh artichokes that my mother used in her *salade de coeurs d'artichauts à l'orange* (page 52). In summer we feasted on zucchini. To this day, I can never get enough of the subtle, pale green vegetable, cooked to a tender consistency and mixed with olive oil and chopped garlic. Summer was also the season to enjoy, on an almost daily basis, what is still my favorite of all Moroccan salads, the savory, cumin-scented egg-plant dish called *zahlouk* (page 71).

SALADE DE COEURS D'ARTICHAUTS À L'ORANGE

◉

ARTICHOKE HEART AND ORANGE SALAD (MOROCCO, ALGERIA)

SERVES 4

MAMAN DARMON, MY GREAT-GRANDMOTHER, USED TO MAKE THIS SALAD WITH SEVILLE ORANGES, THE SOUR ONES USED FOR MAKING MARMALADE, BUT THIS RECIPE USES SWEET NAVEL OR VALENCIA ORANGES. USE ONLY THE ARTICHOKE HEARTS FOR THIS DISH. RESERVE THE LEAVES AND SERVE THEM ON ANOTHER OCCASION WITH A SAVORY DIP.

4 artichokes (about 2 pounds)

1 lemon, halved crosswise

4 oranges

6 radishes, thinly sliced

12 Kalamata olives

2 tablespoons extra-virgin olive oil

½ teaspoon sweet paprika

Salt to taste

In a large pan of boiling water, cook the artichokes and half a lemon, covered, until the artichokes are barely tender, 20 to 25 minutes. Drain and set aside to cool. Pull off the artichoke leaves and cut the fuzzy choke out of each artichoke. Slice the hearts into ¼-inch wedges and set aside.

Squeeze the juice of the other lemon half and set aside. Over a large bowl, peel and section the oranges, discarding the seeds and the white pith.

To serve, alternate the orange sections and artichoke wedges on individual plates. Garnish with radish slices and olives. Mix the olive oil with the lemon juice. Drizzle over the salad. Sprinkle with paprika and salt.

CHALADA DRA

AÏCHA'S CORN SALAD (MOROCCO)

SERVES 6

—

DURING ONE OF MY VISITS TO MARRAKECH I BUMPED INTO AN OLD FRIEND, SAÏD, THE OWNER OF A LARGE BAZAAR NEAR THE CITY'S FAMED DJEMAA EL FNAA SQUARE. HE GRACIOUSLY INVITED ME TO AN IMPROMPTU LUNCH AT HIS HOME. THE MEAL STRETCHED WELL INTO THE AFTERNOON. IT BEGAN WITH AN ASSORTMENT OF SALADS, ONE OF WHICH WAS SO UNUSUAL AND IMAGINATIVE THAT I KNEW I SIMPLY HAD TO GET THE RECIPE. AT THE END OF THE MEAL, SAÏD INTRODUCED ME TO HIS COOK AÏCHA. SHE WAS FLATTERED BY MY REQUEST, AND PROVIDED ME WITH THE LIST OF INGREDIENTS THAT WENT INTO HER SALAD.

Over a large bowl, peel the grapefruit with a knife: Cut down to the flesh, then cut between the membranes, discarding the seeds and the white pith, reserving the juice. Cut each grapefruit section into 1-inch pieces. Combine the grapefruit, corn kernels, radishes, bell pepper, celery, and green onions. Set aside. In a small bowl, whisk together the grapefruit juice, oil, paprika, cumin, salt, and cayenne. Pour over the salad and mix well. Chill for 30 minutes.

Just before serving, peel and dice the apple and the banana. Add them, along with the chopped cilantro, to the other ingredients. Mix well. Garnish with cilantro leaves and serve.

2 pink grapefruit

4 ears of corn, cooked and kernels cut off the cob, or one 15-ounce can corn kernels, drained

6 radishes, finely diced

1 tablespoon minced red bell pepper

4 celery stalks, finely diced

3 green onions with tops, finely sliced

3 tablespoons olive oil

½ teaspoon sweet paprika

2 teaspoons ground cumin

Salt and cayenne to taste

1 tart apple

1 firm ripe banana

10 fresh cilantro sprigs, coarsely chopped

Fresh cilantro leaves for garnish

SALADE DE LENTILLES

LENTIL SALAD (MOROCCO)

SERVES 4

JUST DOWN THE STREET FROM THE APARTMENT WHERE I GREW UP IN THE CENTER OF CASABLANCA, A HANDFUL OF CAFÉS SPECIALIZE IN GRILLED SHISH KABOBS SPRINKLED WITH CUMIN AND SALT. AS A SIDE DISH, THEY OFFER THIS DELICIOUS LENTIL SALAD. IT CAN BE SERVED HOT OR AT ROOM TEMPERATURE.

5 cups vegetable broth (page 23)
   or water

1 cup lentils, rinsed and picked over

5 garlic cloves, coarsely chopped

2 tomatoes (12 ounces), seeded and
   cubed

1 teaspoon dried oregano leaves

20 fresh cilantro sprigs, tied with
   cotton string

2 teaspoons ground turmeric

1 onion

4 whole cloves

2 teaspoons ground cumin

1 teaspoon sweet paprika

⅛ teaspoon cayenne

Salt to taste

Fresh cilantro leaves for garnish

In a large saucepan or a soup pot, combine the broth or water with the lentils, garlic, tomatoes, oregano, cilantro, and turmeric. Stud the onion with the cloves and add it to the mixture. Bring to a rolling boil and cook for 2 minutes. Reduce the heat to medium low. Cover and simmer until the lentils are tender, 20 to 25 minutes.

Discard the onion and cilantro. Remove the lentils from the heat and stir in the cumin, paprika, cayenne, and salt. Garnish with cilantro leaves and serve hot or at room temperature.

CHOU-FLEUR ET COURGETTES EN SALADE

CAULIFLOWER AND ZUCCHINI SALAD (MOROCCO, ALGERIA)

SERVES 4

THE COMBINATION OF ZUCCHINI AND CAULIFLOWER IS PARTICULARLY POPULAR IN MOROCCO AND ALGERIA. THE ZUCCHINI MOST COMMON IN NORTH AFRICA IS ONE WITH A SMOOTH, PALE GREEN SKIN, WHICH I SOMETIMES FIND AT MY LOCAL FARMER'S MARKET IN VISTA, CALIFORNIA. BUT ANY VARIETY WILL WORK WELL FOR THIS DISH.

In a medium skillet over medium-high heat, heat 2 tablespoons of the oil. Place the zucchini in a single layer on the bottom of the pan. Cook until lightly browned on both sides. Drain well on paper towels.

Meanwhile, place the cauliflower and water to cover in a large saucepan. Add the lemon and cook the cauliflower until it is tender, 10 to 15 minutes. Transfer to a colander to drain. Let cool, then mash it coarsely with a fork.

In a serving bowl, combine the zucchini slices with the cauliflower. Toss with the garlic, parsley, lemon juice, salt, and pepper. Sprinkle with paprika and serve.

3 tablespoons olive oil

1 pound small zucchini, cut into ¼-inch-thick slices

1 cauliflower, broken into florets

½ lemon

2 garlic cloves, minced

12 fresh flat-leaf parsley sprigs, minced

2 tablespoons fresh lemon juice

Salt and freshly ground black pepper to taste

1 teaspoon sweet paprika

OMMOK HOURIA

MOTHER HOURIA'S CARROT SALAD (TUNISIA)

SERVES 4

OMMOK HOURIA, OR MOTHER HOURIA, QUITE POSSIBLY THE MOST WELL-KNOWN SALAD IN TUNISIA, APPEARS ON EVERY TABLE, WHETHER IN PRIVATE HOMES OR IN RESTAURANTS. TOPPINGS FOR THIS DISH VARY, FROM CANNED SARDINES AND FLAKES OF TUNA FISH, TO OLIVES AND CAPERS. TUNISIANS LIKE THEIR **OMMOK HOURIA** HOT! THEY BLEND IT LIBERALLY WITH HARISSA. YOU, HOWEVER, MAY PREFER TO ADD HARISSA TO TASTE.

1 pound carrots, peeled and thinly sliced

2 cups water

12 fresh flat-leaf parsley sprigs, minced

1 teaspoon ground caraway

2 tablespoons olive oil

3 tablespoons red wine vinegar

2 garlic cloves, minced

Salt and freshly ground black pepper
*   to taste*

Harissa to taste (page 19)

12 Kalamata or niçoise olives

2 hard-cooked eggs, quartered

In a medium saucepan, bring the water to a boil. Add the carrots, reduce the heat to low, cover, and cook until the carrots are tender, 10 to 15 minutes. Drain. Transfer them to a medium bowl. Add the parsley, caraway, olive oil, vinegar, garlic, salt, pepper, and harissa. Stir well to blend.

To serve, make a mound of *Ommok Houria* on a plate. Stud it with the olives and garnish it with the hard-cooked eggs. Serve at room temperature.

SALADE DE FENOUIL ET PAMPLEMOUSSE

FENNEL AND GRAPEFRUIT SALAD (MOROCCO, ALGERIA)

SERVES 6

I FIND THIS UNUSUAL SALAD QUITE DELICIOUS, ALTHOUGH SOME OF MY AMERICAN FRIENDS HAVE TOLD ME THAT IT IS AN ACQUIRED TASTE. IN MOROCCO, THE MORE EXOTIC BLOOD ORANGES ARE USED WHEN THEY ARE IN SEASON. HOWEVER, I PREFER SWEET RUBY RED GRAPEFRUIT FOR THIS RECIPE.

2 ruby red grapefruit

1 teaspoon salt

1 fennel bulb (about 1 pound)

3 green onions with tops, finely sliced

½ teaspoon ground cumin

3 tablespoons extra-virgin olive oil

12 Kalamata olives

Over a large bowl, peel the grapefruit with a knife: Cut down to the flesh, then cut between the membranes, discarding the seeds and the white pith, reserving the juice. Cut each grapefruit section into 1-inch pieces. Transfer to a serving bowl. Sprinkle with the salt and set aside.

Cut off and discard the woody stems and fronds from the fennel bulb. Slice the bulb crosswise into thin rings. Combine them with the grapefruit. Add the green onions, cumin, and olive oil. Garnish with the olives and serve.

AUBERGINE À L'AIL

GARLICKY EGGPLANT SALAD (TUNISIA)

SERVES 4

SOMETIMES THE SIMPLEST PREPARATION CAN BE THE MOST FLAVORFUL. THIS SALAD, WHICH WAS PART OF AN ELEGANT SEASIDE BUFFET AT THE SHERATON HOTEL IN HAMMAMET, TUNISIA, PROVES THAT POINT. AMONG THE MANY SALADS I TASTED THERE, THIS ONE BROUGHT ME BACK FOR A SECOND AND EVEN A THIRD HELPING. FLAKES OF CANNED TUNA FISH, AS WELL AS A FEW CAPERS, USUALLY COMPLEMENT THE EGGPLANT. MOST TUNISIANS, OF COURSE, ADD A HEALTHY DOLLOP OF HARISSA.

Cut the unpeeled eggplant into large cubes. Sprinkle them with salt and let stand for 10 minutes on a clean towel. Pat dry.

In a large skillet over medium-high heat, heat the olive oil. Fry the eggplant, stirring occasionally, until tender and golden on all the unpeeled sides, 10 to 12 minutes. Stir in the garlic and cook for 1 or 2 minutes. Place the eggplant in a colander to drain for at least 30 minutes.

Lightly pat the eggplant dry with paper towels and transfer it to a serving bowl. Before serving, toss the eggplant with the pepper, vinegar, and parsley. Garnish with capers if desired, and serve with harissa on the side.

1 large globe eggplant

Salt for sprinkling

2 tablespoons olive oil

4 garlic cloves, minced

Freshly ground black pepper to taste

1 tablespoon red wine vinegar

8 fresh flat-leaf parsley sprigs, minced

1 tablespoon capers, drained (optional)

Harissa (page 19) to taste

MATISHA MAHSHEEVA

STUFFED TOMATOES À LA CASABLANCAISE (MOROCCO)

SERVES 6

IN SEASON, YOU WILL FIND STUFFED TOMATOES LIKE THESE ON THE MENU OF MANY OF THE SMALL RESTAURANTS THAT LINE THE FASHIONABLE CORNICHE, THE WIDE BOULEVARD THAT HUGS THE CASABLANCA OCEANFRONT. I SOMETIMES USE CRISP JÍCAMA INSTEAD OF RADISHES IN THIS RECIPE.

With a sharp knife, cut off about ½ inch of the stem end of each tomato. Set aside. With a spoon, scoop out the insides, reserving the pulp. Sprinkle the cavity of each tomato with a little salt and turn the tomatoes upside down in a colander to drain. Finely dice the reserved tomato pulp and set aside.

In a medium skillet over medium high heat, heat 2 tablespoons of the olive oil and cook the onion and the carrots, stirring occasionally, until almost caramelized, 15 to 20 minutes. Set aside to cool.

In a medium saucepan, bring the broth to a boil. Add the rice, stir, and cover. Reduce the heat to medium and cook until the rice is tender, 12 to 15 minutes. Transfer the cooked rice to a medium bowl and fluff it with a fork. Let cool completely. Stir in the remaining 1 tablespoon olive oil. Add the cooked vegetables, reserved tomato pulp, parsley, radishes, bell pepper, preserved lemon rind, cayenne, lemon juice, salt, and pepper. Stuff each tomato with equal amounts of the mixture and top with the reserved stem end. Chill until ready to serve.

6 tomatoes

Salt for sprinkling

3 tablespoons olive oil

1 large onion, finely diced

2 carrots, peeled and finely diced

2 cups vegetable broth (page 23)

1 cup long-grain rice

15 fresh flat-leaf parsley sprigs, coarsely chopped

4 radishes, finely diced

1 tablespoon finely diced red bell pepper

1 teaspoon diced preserved lemon rind (page 15)

⅛ to ¼ teaspoon cayenne

2 tablespoons fresh lemon juice

Salt and freshly ground black pepper to taste

SALADE DE CONCOMBRES ET TOMATES

CUCUMBER AND TOMATO SALAD (MOROCCO, ALGERIA, TUNISIA)

SERVES 4 TO 6

THIS CRUNCHY BLEND OF FINELY DICED CUCUMBERS, ONIONS, AND TOMATOES IS ENJOYED THROUGHOUT NORTH AFRICA. IN MOROCCO, THE COMBINATION MIGHT INCLUDE SOME FINELY DICED PRESERVED LEMON RIND (PAGE 15). IN TUNISIA, A PINCH OF **TABIL** (PAGE 22) SERVES AS THE SEASONING, WHILE ALGERIANS FAVOR A SALAD GARNISHED WITH CHOPPED MINT. **FEQQOUS**, A SLENDER, PRACTICALLY SEEDLESS CUCUMBER, SIMILAR TO JAPANESE OR HOTHOUSE CUCUMBERS, IS THE MOST COMMON VARIETY FOUND IN NORTH AFRICA.

2 cucumbers

Salt for sprinkling

6 tomatoes

4 green onions with tops, finely chopped

2 radishes, finely diced

½ red bell pepper, seeded, deribbed, and finely diced

15 fresh flat-leaf parsley sprigs, minced

1 teaspoon tabil *(page 22), or*

1 tablespoon finely diced preserved lemon rind (page 15)

1 tablespoon fresh lemon juice

2 tablespoons olive oil

Freshly ground black pepper to taste

12 Kalamata or niçoise olives for garnish

Peel, seed, and finely dice 1 cucumber. Sprinkle it with a little salt and set aside in a colander to drain. Peel the remaining cucumber and cut it in half lengthwise. Cut both halves into ¼-inch-thick crosswise slices. Set aside. Cut 3 of the tomatoes in half. Cut each half into ¼-inch-thick crosswise slices, then cut each slice in half. Set aside. Finely dice the remaining tomatoes and add them to the diced cucumber. Drain for 30 minutes.

Transfer the diced cucumber and tomatoes to a large bowl and mix them with the green onions, radishes, bell pepper, parsley, *tabil* or preserved lemon rind, lemon juice, olive oil, and pepper. Toss the vegetables well and chill. Ten minutes before serving, spoon equal amounts of diced vegetables onto the center of individual salad plates. Arrange the half slices of tomato and cucumber around the perimeter of each plate as if they were petals of a flower. Garnish with the olives and serve.

MECHWYA

GRILLED PEPPER SALAD (TUNISIA)

SERVES 6 TO 8

VARIATIONS OF **MECHWYA**, A GRILLED PEPPER SALAD, EXIST THROUGHOUT THE MAGHREB. IN MOROCCO AND ALGERIA IT IS CALLED **CHLADA FELFLA**. THE PEPPERS ARE TRADITIONALLY ROASTED OVER AN OPEN FLAME. THIS CAN BE DONE ON AN OUTDOOR GRILL, OR OVER A GAS BURNER. I FIND IT JUST AS EASY TO GRILL THEM UNDER THE BROILER. I LIKE TO MIX RED, GREEN, AND YELLOW PEPPERS TO CREATE A MORE COLORFUL DISH. CAPERS AND BLACK OLIVES ARE THE MOST COMMON GARNISHES IN TUNISIAN MECHWYA.

Preheat the oven to 350°F. Separate the garlic into cloves, but do not peel them. Place them in a medium baking dish and bake until tender, 25 to 30 to minutes. Let cool and squeeze the pulp out of each clove. Mash it coarsely with a fork and set aside.

Preheat the broiler. Place the peppers and tomatoes on a lightly greased baking sheet about 3 inches from the heat source. Broil the peppers and the tomatoes, turning them carefully with tongs, until the skins are blackened evenly all over. Place the peppers in a paper or plastic bag and close it. When the peppers are cool enough to handle, peel and seed them. Mince them almost to the consistency of a puree. Peel and seed the tomatoes. Finely chop them and add them to the peppers. Place in a colander to drain.

Meanwhile, broil the onion slices in the same manner until soft and golden, 3 or 4 minutes on each side. Finely chop them and set aside.

Place the peppers and the tomatoes in a serving bowl. Stir in the onion, garlic, salt, lemon juice, olive oil, and *tabil*. Garnish with the hard-cooked eggs, capers, and olives.

1 whole garlic bulb

4 large bell peppers

4 large tomatoes

1 large onion, peeled and cut into
½-inch-thick crosswise slices

Salt to taste

3 tablespoons fresh lemon juice

1 tablespoon olive oil

1 teaspoon tabil (page 22)

2 hard-cooked eggs, quartered

Drained capers and Kalamata or niçoise
olives for garnish

ASSIETTE TUNISIENNE

TUNISIAN SALAD PLATE

SERVES 4

THE FRESH FLAVORS OF **ASSIETTE TUNISIENNE** MAY BRING TO MIND A FRENCH **SALADE NIÇOISE**. IN TUNISIA, PRESENTATIONS VARY AS MUCH AS THE INGREDIENTS. SOMETIMES THE SLICED VEGETABLES ARE SET ARTFULLY ON INDIVIDUAL PLATES. ON OTHER OCCASIONS, THE VEGETABLES ARE UNIFORMLY DICED AND GARNISHED WITH CAPERS AND BLACK OLIVES, OR TOPPED WITH A CHUNK OF CANNED TUNA.

3 large tomatoes, peeled, seeded
  (page 24), and sliced
2 green bell peppers, seeded, deribbed,
  and sliced into thin rings
1 cucumber, peeled, seeded, and sliced
1 sweet white onion, thinly sliced and
  separated into rings
2 hard-cooked eggs, shelled and quartered
2 tablespoons red wine vinegar
1 tablespoon water
1 teaspoon Dijon mustard
½ cup extra-virgin olive oil
Salt and freshly ground black pepper
  to taste
1 tablespoon capers, drained
8 Kalamata or niçoise olives

Layer the tomatoes on a serving platter. Cover with layers of pepper rings, cucumber slices, and onion rings. Arrange the eggs around the platter. In a small bowl, whisk the vinegar, water, and mustard together until smooth. Gradually whisk in the olive oil. Season with salt and pepper. Pour the dressing over the salad. Sprinkle with capers and garnish with olives.

CHLADA FELFLA

PEPPER SALAD WITH PRESERVED LEMON (MOROCCO)

SERVES 8

PRESERVED LEMONS, UNIQUE TO NORTH AFRICAN CUISINE, HELP GIVE THIS WONDERFUL SALAD ITS DISTINCTIVE FLAVOR. PRESERVED LEMONS ARE AVAILABLE IN SOME ETHNIC MARKETS IN LARGER CITIES, OR YOU CAN MAKE YOUR OWN.

8 large bell peppers

2 tablespoons olive oil

2 garlic cloves, minced

2 teaspoons preserved lemon rind
   (page 15), very finely diced

2 teaspoons ground cumin

Salt and freshly ground black pepper
   to taste

Fresh lemon juice to taste

Preheat the broiler. Place the peppers on a lightly greased baking sheet about 3 inches from the heat source. Broil the peppers, turning them carefully with tongs, until the skins blacken evenly. Place them in a paper or plastic bag and close it. When the peppers are cool enough to handle, peel, seed, and finely dice them. Place them in a colander to drain, then transfer them to a serving bowl and stir in all the remaining ingredients. Chill until ready to serve.

SLATA BESLA

GRILLED ONION SALAD (TUNISIA)

SERVES 4

SLATA BESLA IS GENERALLY MADE WITH THE MILDER AND SWEETER RED, OR SPANISH, ONIONS. I PREFER, HOWEVER, TO USE ANY OF THE SWEET ONION VARIETIES NOW ON THE MARKET, SUCH AS CALIFORNIA-GROWN SWEET IMPERIALS, OR THE DELICIOUS VIDALIAS, VISALIAS, WALLA WALLAS, OR MAUI ONIONS. YOU CAN GRILL THE ONION SLICES OVER A CHARCOAL FIRE, AS THE TUNISIANS DO, OR GRILL THEM UNDER THE BROILER AS IN THIS RECIPE.

Preheat the broiler. Brush the onion slices lightly with olive oil on both sides. Place them on a baking sheet and broil about 3 inches from the heat source, turning them with tongs, until lightly browned, about 3 or 4 minutes on each side. Transfer to a shallow bowl and separate into rings. Toss with the remaining olive oil and the remaining ingredients. Serve immediately.

4 sweet onions, cut into ½-inch
   crosswise slices
3 tablespoons olive oil
1 tablespoon fresh lemon juice
1 tablespoon capers, drained
Salt and freshly ground black pepper
   to taste

CHAKCHOUKA

FRIED PEPPER SALAD (TUNISIA)

SERVES 4

IN TUNISIA, THERE ARE AS MANY RECIPES FOR **CHAKCHOUKA** AS THERE ARE COOKS. THE DIFFERENCE BETWEEN CHAKCHOUKA AND **MECHWYA**, WHICH SHARE MANY OF THE SAME INGREDIENTS, IS THAT THE VEGETABLES IN THE FORMER ARE LIGHTLY FRIED RATHER THAN GRILLED, AS THEY ARE IN THE LATTER. FOR MY FRIEND MEHERZIA JAZIRI, THE SECRET TO A GOOD CHAKCHOUKA IS TO NOT OVERCOOK IT, OR AS SHE LIKES TO SAY: "YOU MUST EAT IT **LIVE!**" TUNISIANS SAVOR **CHAKCHOUKA** PLAIN OR TOPPED WITH CHUNKS OF SPICY MERGUEZ SAUSAGE. EGGS COOKED IN A NEST OF **CHAKCHOUKA** MAKE A WONDERFUL BRUNCH ENTREE. FIRM PLUM TOMATOES ARE THE PREFERRED VARIETY FOR THIS RECIPE.

2 tablespoons olive oil

2 large onions, thinly sliced

1 pound plum (Roma) tomatoes, cubed

Harissa to taste (page 19)

2 green bell peppers, seeded, deribbed,
*   and diced*

2 red or yellow bell peppers, seeded,
*   deribbed, and diced*

3 mild Anaheim chilies, seeded, deribbed,
*   and diced*

8 to 10 garlic cloves, coarsely chopped

4 eggs (optional)

Salt and freshly ground black pepper
*   to taste*

1 teaspoon tabil (page 22)

In a large skillet over medium heat, heat the olive oil and cook the onions, stirring occasionally, until golden, 10 to 12 minutes. Reduce the heat to medium low and add the tomatoes and harissa. Cook, stirring occasionally, until the tomatoes attain the consistency of a chunky puree, 20 to 25 minutes. Stir in the peppers, chilies, and garlic. Cover and cook, stirring occasionally, until the peppers are tender, 10 to 15 minutes.

If adding eggs, make several depressions in the *chakchouka,* with the back of a large spoon, after it has cooked for 10 to 12 minutes. Break an egg into each depression. Cover and cook 5 to 6 minutes longer, or until the whites are set. Remove from the heat and season with salt, pepper, and *tabil.*

Serve *chakchouka* with eggs immediately, accompanied with crusty bread. Serve eggless *chakchouka* at room temperature.

SLATA KRAA

FATMA'S ZUCCHINI SALAD (TUNISIA)

SERVES 4

MY FRIEND FATMA IS A BUSY TUNISIAN CAREER WOMAN WHO STILL FINDS TIME TO SPEND IN HER KITCHEN. SHE SERVES THIS REFRESHING SALAD DURING THE SUMMER MONTHS WHEN **KRAA**, A LOCAL VARIETY OF ZUCCHINI WITH A PALE GREEN SKIN, IS IN SEASON. NO MATTER HOW MUCH SHE MAKES, IT NEVER SEEMS TO BE ENOUGH, SHE SAYS WITH A LAUGH. THE FLAVOR OF BLACK PEPPER AND DRIED MINT SHOULD BE QUITE PRONOUNCED. MEMBERS OF FATMA'S FAMILY ENJOY MIXING CHUNKS OF CANNED TUNA AND LOTS OF PIQUANT HARISSA WITH THEIR SALAD. IT IS TRADITIONALLY SERVED CHILLED.

Cut the zucchini into thin crosswise slices. In a medium saucepan, combine them with the water. Bring to a boil, and cook, covered, until the zucchini is tender, 10 to 15 minutes. Transfer to a colander to drain.

Place the zucchini in a serving bowl and mash it with a fork to get a lumpy puree. Add the garlic, salt, pepper, mint, vinegar, and olive oil. Mix well. Sprinkle with capers. Serve with harissa on the side, if you like.

2 pounds zucchini

1 cup water

2 teaspoons minced garlic

*Salt and freshly ground black pepper
  to taste*

2 teaspoons dried mint leaves, crushed

2 tablespoons red wine vinegar

3 tablespoons olive oil

1 tablespoon capers, drained

Harissa (page 19), (optional)

SALADE DE POMMES DE TERRE AU CUMIN

PIEDS-NOIRS POTATO SALAD (ALGERIA)

SERVES 4 TO 6

MY BROTHER BRIAN, A PIEDS-NOIRS LIKE ME, NOW LIVES IN CANADA AND FREQUENTLY PREPARES THIS NORTH AFRICAN POTATO SALAD FOR HIS FAMILY. IT IS A WONDERFUL PICNIC DISH. IF SWEET ONIONS ARE NOT IN SEASON, USE GREEN ONIONS INSTEAD.

*1 pound small potatoes, peeled and
    quartered*
*2 large tomatoes, peeled, seeded,
    and diced*
1 sweet onion, very finely diced
2 teaspoons ground cumin
3 tablespoons olive oil
1 tablespoon red wine vinegar
10 green olives, pitted and sliced
*Salt and freshly ground black pepper
    to taste*
12 fresh cilantro sprigs, minced

In a large pan of boiling water, cook the potatoes until tender, 15 to 20 minutes. Drain well. While the potatoes are still warm, place them in a salad bowl and mix them with the tomatoes, onion, cumin, olive oil, vinegar, olives, salt, and pepper. Toss with the cilantro before serving.

AZIZA'S ZAHLOUK

EGGPLANT SALAD (MOROCCO)

SERVES 4

Aziza Rharrit, a friend from Casablanca, is standing at her kitchen stove wrapped in a fragrant cloud of cumin-scented steam. She is preparing **zahlouk**, one of Morocco's most popular salads. She likes to serve it on a bed of lettuce, as part of a trio of salads that might include garlic-flavored cooked carrots and a colorful blend of diced tomatoes and cucumbers (page 62). The flavor of **zahlouk** is greatly enhanced by using vine-ripened tomatoes.

Preheat the oven to 375°F. Peel and coarsely cube the eggplant. Place the cubes on a kitchen towel and sprinkle them with salt. Let them stand for 15 minutes, then gently pat them dry. In a 2-quart ovenproof baking dish, place the eggplant, tomato paste, tomatoes, paprika, cumin, olive oil, and garlic. Sprinkle with sugar. Mix all the ingredients well. Cover with aluminum foil, and cook until the eggplant is completely tender, 45 to 50 minutes. Stir once or twice while baking. If the mixture becomes too dry, add a little water.

Place the mixture in a serving dish and season with salt and pepper. Stir in enough lemon juice to obtain a light, tangy taste. To serve, spoon the *zahlouk* onto a bed of lettuce and garnish with black olives.

1 small globe eggplant

Salt for sprinkling

One 6-ounce can tomato paste

2 large tomatoes, cubed

2 teaspoons sweet paprika

1 teaspoon ground cumin

2 tablespoons olive oil

2 garlic cloves, minced

½ teaspoon sugar

Freshly ground black pepper to taste

Fresh lemon juice to taste

Lettuce leaves for serving

10 black olives for garnish

chapter three

EGG DISHES

EGG DISHES

COOKS THROUGHOUT THE MAGHREB MAKE WONDERFUL USE OF EGGS. THIS IS ESPECIALLY TRUE IN TUNISIA. THERE, A THICK, CRUSTLESS QUICHE CALLED A **MAKHOUDA** IS SERVED DAILY IN MANY HOUSEHOLDS. The *makhouda*, which is baked in the oven, resembles an Italian frittata filled with small bits of meat or seafood, diced vegetables, cheese, and herbs. The popularity of this "Tunisian omelet," as we used to call it when I was growing up, has spread throughout the Maghreb.

In both *ojja* and *testira,* two other Tunisian specialties, the eggs are stirred into the vegetables and cooked on top of the stove to create a delectable dish similar to a Basque *pipérade.* Although you can serve these elaborate yet inexpensive egg and vegetable creations as a first course, you can also make them the focal point of the meal by serving them with a side dish or a salad and lots of warm, crusty bread.

MAKHOUDA AUX ÉPINARDS

CRUSTLESS SPINACH QUICHE (TUNISIA)

SERVES 6

ON A SUNNY MORNING IN GAMMARTH, TUNISIA, MEHERZIA JAZIRI IS BUSTLING AROUND HER TIDY KITCHEN, PREPARING ONE OF HER FAMILY'S FAVORITE **MAKHOUDAS**. SHE EXPLAINS ALMOST APOLOGETICALLY THAT MAKHOUDA ISN'T CONSIDERED ELEGANT ENOUGH TO SERVE TO GUESTS, SINCE IT CONTAINS NO MEAT. I HEARTILY DISAGREE, TELLING HER ABOUT THE CURRENT TREND IN VEGETARIAN CUISINE NOW SWEEPING ACROSS THE UNITED STATES. THIS DISH CALLS FOR A PINCH OF **BHARAT**, AN INTRIGUING BLEND OF DRIED ROSE PETALS, CINNAMON, AND BLACK PEPPER.

Preheat the oven to 400°F. In a medium skillet over medium-high heat, heat the oil and cook the onion, stirring occasionally, until it is almost caramelized, 10 to 12 minutes. Add the spinach and cook until just wilted. Stir in the parsley and set aside. In a large bowl, beat the eggs and add the Parmesan cheese, Swiss or Gruyère cheese, *bharat*, bread crumbs, baking powder, and salt. Stir in the spinach mixture.

Generously grease a 2-quart soufflé dish. Pour the egg mixture into the dish and bake on the middle rack until golden brown and firm, 45 to 50 minutes, or until knife inserted in the center comes out clean. Let cool for 10 minutes before unmolding onto a serving platter. Cut into wedges or small cubes. Serve at room temperature with lemon wedges on the side.

2 tablespoons olive oil

1 onion, finely diced

*1 pound fresh spinach, stemmed and
    coarsely chopped*

30 fresh flat-leaf parsley sprigs, minced

8 eggs

*½ cup (2 ounces) freshly grated
    Parmesan cheese*

*4 ounces Swiss or Gruyère cheese, cut
    into ¼-inch cubes*

2 teaspoons bharat *(page 21)*

½ cup dried bread crumbs

½ teaspoon baking powder

Salt to taste

Lemon wedges

MAKHOUDA MECHWYA

CRUSTLESS GRILLED PEPPER QUICHE (TUNISIA)

SERVES 6 TO 8

THIS **MAKHOUDA** IS MADE WITH **MECHWYA,** THE TUNISIAN GRILLED PEPPER SALAD (PAGE 63). SERVE IT HOT OR COLD. I LIKE TO USE IT AS A SANDWICH FILLING.

8 eggs

1 cup mechwya (page 63)

4 ounces Swiss or Gruyère cheese, cut
    into ¼-inch cubes

¼ cup (1 ounce) freshly grated
    Parmesan cheese

2 tablespoons dried bread crumbs

2 teaspoons sweet paprika

1 tablespoon diced preserved lemon rind
    (page 15)

Lemon wedges for garnish

Preheat the oven to 400°F. In a large bowl, beat the eggs and add the *mechwya*, cubed and grated cheeses, bread crumbs, paprika, and preserved lemon. Set aside.

Generously grease a 2-quart soufflé dish. Pour the egg mixture into the dish and bake on the middle rack until golden brown and firm, 45 to 50 minutes, or until a knife inserted in the center comes out clean. Let cool for 10 minutes before unmolding onto a serving platter. Cut into wedges or small cubes. Serve at room temperature with lemon wedges on the side.

MAKHOUDA NAHNA

CRUSTLESS QUICHE WITH MINT (TUNISIA)

SERVES 4 TO 6

MASHED NAVY BEANS GIVE THIS **MAKHOUDA** AN UNUSUAL TEXTURE. THE FLAVOR OF DRIED MINT SHOULD BE QUITE PRONOUNCED. SERVE IT HOT OR AT ROOM TEMPERATURE. LIKE MOST **MAKHOUDAS,** IT CAN BE SLICED AND USED AS A FILLING FOR SANDWICHES.

Preheat the oven to 400°F. In a medium skillet over medium-high heat, heat the oil and cook the onion, stirring occasionally, until lightly browned, 8 to 10 minutes. Set aside. In a large bowl, beat the eggs and add the onion, beans, parsley, mint, cheese, bread crumbs, paprika, *bharat,* and salt.

Generously grease a 2-quart soufflé dish. Pour the egg mixture into the dish and bake on the middle rack until golden brown and firm, 45 to 50 minutes, or until a knife inserted in the center comes out clean. Let cool for 10 minutes before unmolding onto a serving platter. Cut into wedges or small cubes. Serve at room temperature with lemon wedges on the side.

2 tablespoons olive oil

1 large onion, finely diced

8 eggs

1 cup canned navy beans, drained and mashed with a fork

20 fresh flat-leaf parsley sprigs, minced

1½ tablespoons dried mint leaves, crushed

8 ounces Swiss or Gruyère cheese, cut into ¼-inch cubes

3 tablespoons dried bread crumbs

1 tablespoon sweet paprika

1 teaspoon bharat *(page 21)*

½ teaspoon salt

Lemon wedges for garnish

MAKHOUDA D'AUBERGINE

CRUSTLESS EGGPLANT QUICHE (TUNISIA)

SERVES 6

SEVERAL YEARS AGO, I SPENT A SUMMER IN CARTHAGE WITH A TUNISIAN FAMILY. MY HOSTESS WOULD OFTEN MAKE THIS DELICIOUS **MAKHOUDA** FOR US TO SNACK ON. I WOULD STUFF A THICK SLICE INSIDE A CRUSTY **PETIT PAIN**, SPREAD IT WITH A LITTLE HARISSA, AND HEAD FOR THE NEARBY BEACH TO SUNBATHE AND ENJOY MY ALFRESCO LUNCH. IT IS IMPORTANT TO DRAIN AS MUCH OIL AS POSSIBLE FROM THE EGGPLANT BEFORE COMBINING IT WITH THE EGGS.

Preheat the oven to 400°F. Peel and cut the eggplant into ¼-inch dice. Sprinkle lightly with salt and place the cubes on a clean towel for 10 minutes. Pat dry with paper towels.

In a medium skillet over medium-high heat, heat the olive oil and cook the eggplant, onion, and pepper, stirring occasionally, until the vegetables are golden, 10 to 12 minutes. Set aside in a colander to drain for at least 30 minutes.

In a medium bowl, mix the eggs and add the parsley, garlic, cheese, and bread crumbs. Add the eggplant mixture. Season with *bharat*, salt, and optional harissa.

Generously grease a 2-quart soufflé dish. Pour the egg mixture into the dish and bake on the middle rack until golden brown, 45 to 50 minutes, or until a knife inserted in the center comes out clean. Let cool for 10 minutes before unmolding onto a serving platter. Cut into wedges or small cubes. Serve hot or at room temperature with lemon wedges on the side.

1 large globe eggplant

Salt for sprinkling

¼ cup olive oil

1 onion, finely diced

½ red bell pepper, seeded, deribbed, and finely diced

8 eggs

20 fresh flat-leaf parsley sprigs, minced

4 garlic cloves, minced

8 ounces Swiss or Gruyère cheese, cut into ¼-inch cubes

½ cup dried bread crumbs

1 teaspoon bharat *(page 21)*

Harissa (page 19), (optional)

Lemon wedges for garnish

OJJA À LA COURGE

TUNISIAN PUMPKIN SCRAMBLE (TUNISIA)

SERVES 4

IN TUNISIA, **OJJA** IS USUALLY TOPPED WITH CHUNKS OF SPICY MERGUEZ SAUSAGE. MEATLESS VERSIONS CALL FOR SMALL CUBES OF POTATO OR WINTER SQUASH, AND SOMETIMES CAULIFLOWER FLORETS. ANY FIRM-FLESHED WINTER SQUASH IS GOOD IN **OJJA**. SERVE IT WITH WARM CRUSTY BREAD.

2 tablespoons olive oil

8 ounces butternut squash, peeled and
   cut into ½-inch dice

5 tomatoes (1¾ pounds), peeled seeded
   (see page 24), and coarsely chopped

1 tablespoon tomato paste

4 garlic cloves, minced

2 bell peppers, seeded, deribbed, and cut
   into ¼-inch-wide strips

Salt and freshly ground black pepper
   to taste

1 teaspoon ground caraway

2 teaspoons harissa (page 19)

6 eggs, lightly beaten

In a large skillet over medium-high heat, heat the oil and cook the squash, stirring occasionally, until lightly browned, 2 to 3 minutes. Add the tomatoes and cook, stirring, until they become a puree, 5 to 6 minutes. Add the tomato paste, garlic, and pepper strips. Lower the heat to medium and continue cooking, stirring occasionally, until the squash is tender, 10 to 15 minutes. Season with salt, pepper, caraway seed, and harissa. A few minutes before serving, add the beaten eggs. Cook, stirring, until the eggs form soft curds. Serve immediately.

TESTIRA

TUNISIAN-STYLE PIPÉRADE

SERVES 4 TO 6

THIS DISH IS TRADITIONALLY SERVED AS AN ACCOMPANIMENT TO GRILLED OR FRIED FISH IN TUNISIA. MY FIRST TASTE OF **TESTIRA** WAS AT CHEZ SLAH, A SMALL RESTAURANT AND FIXTURE OF CENTRAL TUNIS FOR OVER THIRTY YEARS. THEIR SPECIALTY IS FRESH SEAFOOD. EACH DISH COMES WITH A SIDE ORDER OF **TESTIRA**, A BLEND OF SCRAMBLED EGGS, GREEN PEPPERS, AND TOMATOES. YOU CAN SERVE **TESTIRA** OVER RICE, OR ON ITS OWN AS A BRUNCH ENTREE WITH CRUSTY BREAD. TUNISIANS, OF COURSE, AREN'T TIMID WHEN IT COMES TO ADDING FIERY HARISSA TO THIS DISH! YOU SHOULD ADD IT TO TASTE, HOWEVER.

Preheat the broiler. Place the peppers, chili, and tomatoes on a lightly greased baking sheet about 3 inches from the heat source. Broil them, turning them carefully with tongs, until the skins are evenly blackened. Set the tomatoes aside to cool. Transfer the peppers to a paper or plastic bag and close it. When the peppers are cool enough to handle, seed, and cut them into 1-inch pieces. When the tomatoes are cool enough to handle, peel, seed, and dice them coarsely.

In a large skillet over medium heat, heat the olive oil and cook the tomatoes, stirring occasionally, until the mixture thickens somewhat, 5 to 6 minutes. Add the peppers and chili, and cook, stirring occasionally, for 10 to 12 minutes. Season with the *tabil*, salt, pepper, and harissa. Add the eggs to the mixture, and stir gently until they are cooked. Serve immediately.

2 red bell peppers

2 green bell peppers

1 fresh New Mexico or Anaheim red or green chili (optional)

4 large tomatoes

2 tablespoons olive oil

2 teaspoons tabil *(page 22)*

Salt and freshly ground black pepper to taste

4 eggs, lightly beaten

1 teaspoon harissa (page 19)

MARKODE AUX POMMES DE TERRE

ALGERIAN-STYLE FRITTATA (ALGERIA)

SERVES 4 TO 6 AS A FIRST COURSE

ALGERIAN **MARKODE** IS A MEATLESS OMELET SIMILAR TO TUNISIAN **MAKHOUDA** AND TO A SPANISH POTATO TORTILLA. IT IS SOMETIMES CUT INTO BITE-SIZED PIECES AND SERVED AS AN APPETIZER. THIS IS ONE THE SEPHARDIC RECIPES HANDED DOWN BY MY GREAT-AUNT SUZANNE CORIAT, OR TITA, AS WE CALLED HER. SHE OFTEN ADDED DICED CARROT AND A HANDFUL OF FRESH GREEN PEAS TO HER **MARKODE**. BECAUSE THE PRESERVED LEMONS USED HERE ARE ALREADY SALTED, IT PROBABLY WON'T BE NECESSARY TO ADD MORE SALT.

3 tablespoons olive oil

2 potatoes (about 1 pound), peeled and
   cut into ¼-inch dice

1 small onion, finely diced

4 garlic cloves, minced

2 teaspoons sweet paprika

6 thawed frozen or canned artichoke
   hearts, drained and coarsely chopped

1 tablespoon minced preserved lemon
   rind (page 15)

8 eggs

15 fresh flat-leaf parsley sprigs, minced

Lemon wedges for garnish

Preheat the oven to 400°F. In a medium skillet over medium heat, heat the oil and add the potatoes, onion, and garlic. Cover and cook until the potatoes are almost tender, 12 to 15 minutes. Add the paprika, artichoke hearts, and preserved lemon rind. Cook, stirring, for 1 to 2 minutes. Set aside. In a medium bowl, beat the eggs with the parsley.

Generously grease a 2-quart soufflé dish. Spoon in the potato mixture and pour the eggs over the top. Bake until a knife inserted in the center comes out clean, 45 to 50 minutes. Let cool for 10 minutes before unmolding onto a serving dish. Cut into wedges or small cubes. Serve with lemon wedges on the side.

NOTE: *Markode* can also be cooked on top of the stove like a Spanish tortilla or an Italian frittata. In a skillet, cook the vegetables, herbs, and spices as directed above. Add the beaten eggs. Cook until the eggs are set on the bottom, taking care not to let them burn. To cook the top, set a large plate over the pan and carefully turn it upside down. Gently slide the *markode* back into the pan and cook until set. Slide the *markode* onto a serving platter. Serve warm with lemon wedges.

CHEF AHMED'S EGGS MALSOUKA

EGG AND SPINACH PIE (TUNISIA)

MAKES 4 INDIVIDUAL PASTRIES

CHEF AHMED OUAILI HAS BEEN OVERSEEING THE BUSY KITCHEN OF THE SHERATON HOTEL IN HIS NATIVE CITY OF HAMMAMET FOR OVER TWO DECADES. AMID HISSING STEAMERS AND DEEP-FAT FRYERS, HE REMEMBERS THE DAYS WHEN HIS MOTHER PREPARED THE FAMILY MEAL OVER A CHARCOAL FIRE. NOWADAYS, THE CHEF CAN BE FOUND EARLY EACH MORNING AT THE ENTRANCE TO HIS CAVERNOUS KITCHENS, AWAITING THE ARRIVAL OF THE DAY'S SUPPLY OF FRESH VEGETABLES FROM NEARBY CAP BON, TUNISIA'S MOST FERTILE AGRICULTURAL REGION.

Chef Ouaili, who often represents Tunisia in international gastronomic events, likes to prepare this dish in individual portions. His recipe calls for a small amount of cubed cooked chicken breast, which I have eliminated from the list of ingredients. The chef maintains that fresh spinach leaves add more body to the filling. I find Chinese egg roll skins good substitutes for *malsouka*, the paper-thin pastry dough used in Tunisia.

In a small skillet over medium-high heat, heat the oil and cook the onion, stirring occasionally, until it is almost caramelized, 10 to 12 minutes. In a large bowl, combine the onion, parsley, spinach, grated and diced cheeses, salt, *bharat*, bread crumbs, coriander, and eggs. Stir until well blended. Set aside.

Preheat the oven to 425°F. Carefully separate the egg roll skins. Place each one on a flat surface and brush it with melted butter. Spoon ¼ cup of the filling onto the center of an egg roll skin. Fold over two opposing sides so that they overlap slightly in the center to just cover the filling. Next, fold over the other two sides to obtain a 3½-inch-square pastry. Brush the pastry on both sides with melted butter and place it, seam-side down, on a nonstick or lightly greased baking sheet. Proceed in the same manner with the remaining egg roll skins. Bake until golden brown, 20 to 25 minutes. Serve hot with lemon wedges on the side.

2 tablespoons olive oil

1 onion, finely diced

15 fresh flat-leaf parsley sprigs, minced

4 lightly packed cups (about 4 ounces) fresh spinach leaves, finely chopped

½ cup (2 ounces) freshly grated Swiss or Gruyère cheese, plus 4 ounces Swiss or Gruyère cheese cut into ¼-inch cubes

1 teaspoon salt

1 teaspoon bharat (page 21)

2 tablespoons dried bread crumbs

½ teaspoon ground coriander

2 eggs, lightly beaten

Four 7-inch-square Chinese egg roll skins

4 tablespoons butter, melted

Lemon wedges for garnish

chapter four

SWEET AND
SAVORY STEWS

SWEET AND SAVORY STEWS

ANYONE WHO HAS TASTED **TAGINES,** THE EXOTIC STEWS OF MOROCCO AND ALGERIA, WILL AGREE THAT THE WORD **STEW** IS HARDLY ADEQUATE TO DESCRIBE THESE DELECTABLE CREATIONS. "A *tagine* is filled with mystery, just like poetry!" says author Edmond Amran El Maleh.

The word *tagine* also refers to the earthenware pot in which the stew is traditionally cooked. The distinctive conical lid of this pot is an ingenious device for capturing and holding the steam during the cooking process. In Morocco and Algeria, a *tagine* is meant to simmer slowly over a small charcoal brazier until the sauce, redolent with cinnamon, saffron, garlic, or preserved lemons, is reduced to its essence and acquires a deep, rich flavor. When serving a *tagine,* the conical lid is removed slowly, to allow the cloud of intensely aromatic steam to wrap around the diners like a warm and fragrant shawl. You may substitute a heavy enameled cast-iron casserole or Dutch oven that can go from oven to table.

TAGINE BATATA HLOOWA

TAGINE OF YAMS AND CARROTS IN HONEY SAUCE (MOROCCO)

SERVES 4 TO 6

ONE OF MOROCCO'S BEST-KNOWN **TAGINES** COMBINES LAMB WITH PRUNES, HONEY, AND SESAME SEEDS. IN THIS MEATLESS VERSION, I HAVE SUBSTITUTED CARROTS AND YAMS FOR THE LAMB. THE VEGETABLES SHOULD ACQUIRE AN ALMOST CARAMELIZED CONSISTENCY IN THE SYRUPY SAUCE. SERVE THIS **TAGINE** WITH LOTS OF WARM, CRUSTY BREAD TO MOP UP THE SAUCE.

Preheat the oven to 400°F. In a large saucepan of boiling water, blanch the onions for 1 minute. Drain and peel. In a heavy enameled cast-iron casserole or a small Dutch oven over medium-high heat, melt the butter with the oil and cook the onions, stirring occasionally, until tender, 6 to 8 minutes.

Remove half of the onions and reserve. Add the yams or sweet potatoes and carrots to the pan. Cook, stirring, until lightly browned. Add the broth, honey, cinnamon, ginger, prunes, salt, and pepper. Stir to blend. Cover with aluminum foil, then with a tight-fitting lid.

Bake until the vegetables are tender, 45 to 50 minutes. Place the reserved onions evenly over the top. Bake for 5 to 10 minutes more. Sprinkle with sesame seeds before serving.

30 pearl onions (about 10 ounces)

2 tablespoons butter

1 tablespoon olive oil

1½ to 2 pounds yams or sweet
    potatoes, peeled and cut into
    1-inch chunks

2 large carrots, peeled and cut into
    chunks

2 cups vegetable broth (page 23)

¼ cup honey

½ teaspoon ground cinnamon

¼ teaspoon ground ginger

1 cup pitted prunes

Salt to taste

1 teaspoon freshly ground black pepper
    to taste

1 tablespoon toasted sesame seeds
    (page 24), for garnish

TAGINE BIL HUMMUS

GARBANZO BEAN AND CARROT STEW (MOROCCO)

SERVES 4

TAGINE BIL HUMMUS IS A COUNTRY-STYLE DISH, SERVED WHEN TIMES ARE HARD AND MEAT IS SCARCE. THE DRIED GARBANZO BEANS ARE USUALLY SOAKED OVERNIGHT AND THE SKINS PAINSTAKINGLY REMOVED BY HAND. CITY COOKS CAN SIMPLY RUN DOWN TO THEIR NEIGHBORHOOD MARKET AND PURCHASE A FEW HUNDRED GRAMS OF PRESOAKED GARBANZO BEANS. I USE CANNED BEANS FOR CONVENIENCE, AND SERVE THIS DISH OVER COUSCOUS.

¼ cup vegetable oil

1 large onion, finely diced

3 garlic cloves, minced

12 fresh cilantro sprigs, minced

½ teaspoon ground turmeric

¾ teaspoon ground cinnamon

½ teaspoon cayenne

3 carrots, peeled and cut into diagonal
  slices, ¼-inch thick

Two 15-ounce cans garbanzo beans,
  drained and liquid reserved

½ teaspoon black pepper

Salt to taste

1 tablespoon smen (page 18), (optional)

Minced fresh cilantro for garnish

In a small enameled cast-iron casserole or a Dutch oven over medium-high heat, heat the oil and cook the onion, stirring occasionally, until tender, 6 to 8 minutes. Add the garlic, cilantro, turmeric, cinnamon, cayenne, carrots, and the reserved liquid from the garbanzo beans. Reduce the heat to medium, cover, and cook until the carrots are tender, 15 to 20 minutes. Add the garbanzo beans, pepper, salt, and optional *smen*. Heat through. Before serving, sprinkle with the cilantro.

TAGINE BATATA, JILBANA, WA KELBKOK

TAGINE OF POTATOES, PEAS, AND ARTICHOKE HEARTS (MOROCCO)

SERVES 4 TO 6

I FIRST TASTED THIS SUCCULENT **TAGINE** IN THE SMALL TOWN OF MOULAY IDRISS, ONE OF MOROCCO'S HOLIEST CITIES, NAMED FOR THE COUNTRY'S PATRON SAINT. SEATED AROUND SMALL TABLES ON THE RESTAURANT'S TERRACE, WE OVERLOOKED THE GREEN-TILED ROOF SHELTERING THE SAINT'S TOMB, WITH THE ANCIENT RUINS OF THE ROMAN TOWN OF VOLUBILIS IN THE DISTANCE. TRADITIONALLY, THE STEMS OF THE ARTICHOKES AS WELL AS THE HEARTS ARE USED IN THIS **TAGINE**. THE STEMS, WHEN PEELED OF THEIR FIBROUS OUTER LAYER, TASTE JUST LIKE THE TENDER HEART.

If using fresh artichokes, place them in a pan of boiling water to which a lemon half has been added. Cook, covered, until base is tender when pierced with a knife. Let cool. Pull off the leaves and cut out the fuzzy choke. Peel the fibrous outer layer from the stems and cut them into 1-inch pieces. Set aside. If using canned artichokes, drain them; if using frozen artichokes, let them thaw. Squeeze the other lemon half and set the juice aside.

In a large bowl, place the parsley, cilantro, saffron, turmeric, and reserved lemon juice. Add the potatoes and stir to coat them. Set aside. In a small Dutch oven or heavy saucepan over medium-high heat, heat the olive oil and cook the onion, stirring occasionally, until tender, 6 to 8 minutes. Reduce the heat to medium and add the potatoes and broth. Cover and cook until the potatoes are almost tender, 12 to 15 minutes.

Add the preserved lemon rind, artichoke hearts, artichoke stems if using, and peas. Season with salt and pepper. Cook until the artichokes are heated through, 8 to 10 minutes.

To serve, place the vegetables on a platter and spoon the sauce over the top. Garnish with the parsley.

6 artichokes, with stems if possible (about 2½ pounds), or one 15-ounce can artichoke hearts, drained, or one 10-ounce package frozen artichoke hearts

1 lemon

12 fresh flat-leaf parsley sprigs, minced

10 fresh cilantro sprigs, minced

6 Spanish saffron threads, crushed

1 teaspoon ground turmeric

1½ pounds boiling potatoes, peeled and cut into large wedges

2 tablespoons olive oil

1 onion, finely diced

1½ cups vegetable broth (page 23)

2 teaspoons finely diced preserved lemon rind (page 15)

One 10-ounce package frozen baby peas

Salt and freshly ground black pepper to taste

Minced fresh flat-leaf parsley sprigs for garnish

KEFTA AUX OEUFS

VEGETARIAN MEATBALLS WITH EGGS IN TOMATO SAUCE (MOROCCO, ALGERIA, TUNISIA)

SERVES 4

KEFTA REFERS TO A MIXTURE OF GROUND MEAT AND FRESH HERBS. SOMETIMES IT IS SHAPED INTO SMALL BALLS AND SIMMERED IN A CINNAMON-SCENTED TOMATO SAUCE, LIKE THE ONE IN THIS RECIPE. ON OTHER OCCASIONS, **KEFTA** IS ROLLED INTO A SAUSAGE SHAPE, SKEWERED, AND GRILLED OR BAKED. THIS VEGETARIAN ADAPTATION IS SERVED AS A LIGHT DINNER OR AS A FIRST COURSE.

Tomato Sauce

One 28-ounce can crushed tomatoes

2 onions, minced

1 teaspoon ground cinnamon

2 teaspoons sugar

10 fresh flat-leaf parsley sprigs

10 fresh cilantro sprigs, minced

½ teaspoon salt

¼ teaspoon freshly ground black pepper

Kefta

10 fresh flat-leaf parsley sprigs, minced

5 fresh cilantro sprigs, minced

1 cup dried bread crumbs

3 eggs

2 tablespoons vegetable oil

1 teaspoon ground cumin

8 fresh mint leaves, minced

2 garlic cloves, minced

½ teaspoon salt

½ teaspoon freshly ground black pepper

4 tablespoons vegetable oil, for frying

4 eggs

Minced fresh flat-leaf parsley for garnish

To make the tomato sauce: In a large saucepan over low heat, combine all the ingredients. Cover and simmer for 40 to 45 minutes. Transfer the sauce to an ovenproof dish.

Meanwhile, to make the kefta: In a large bowl, combine all the ingredients, except the oil for frying, the eggs, and the parsley. Mix, using your hands, until you obtain a homogeneous mixture. Form heaping teaspoonfuls into small balls about ¾ inch in diameter.

Preheat the oven to 400°F. In a large, seasoned cast-iron or nonstick skillet over medium-high heat, heat the vegetable oil and fry the balls, in batches if necessary, until evenly brown, about 4 or 5 minutes. With a slotted spoon, place them on paper towels to drain. Carefully transfer the balls to the tomato sauce. Break the eggs over them, keeping the yolks whole. Bake until the eggs are set and the yolks somewhat runny, 8 to 10 minutes. Sprinkle with the minced parsley and serve immediately.

DJAJA TARAT

LENTILS WITH YAMS (MOROCCO)

SERVES 6

IN THE MAGHREB, HOME-STYLE DISHES LIKE THIS ONE ARE TYPICALLY SERVED IN THE WINTER MONTHS. THIS RECIPE WAS INSPIRED BY ONE CITED IN **LA CUISINE MAROCAINE DE RABAT** (THE CAPITAL OF MOROCCO), BY HAYAT DINIA, FOR A TRADITIONAL MOROCCAN DISH CALLED **DJAJA TARAT** (WHICH MEANS "THE CHICKEN FLEW AWAY!"). PUMPKIN OR BUTTERNUT SQUASH ARE DELICIOUS ALTERNATIVES TO YAMS. YOU CAN ALSO SUBSTITUTE GARBANZO BEANS FOR THE LENTILS.

6 cups vegetable broth (page 23)

6 Spanish saffron threads, crushed

1 teaspoon ground turmeric

1 cup lentils, rinsed and picked over

1 large onion, finely chopped

20 fresh cilantro sprigs, tied with
   cotton string

2 carrots, peeled and finely diced

1 yam, peeled and cut into ¼-inch dice

3 tablespoons tomato paste

1 teaspoon ground ginger

Salt and freshly ground black pepper
   to taste

10 fresh flat-leaf parsley sprigs, minced,
   for garnish

In a large saucepan or a soup pot, combine the broth, saffron, turmeric, lentils, onion, and cilantro. Bring to a rolling boil and cook for 2 minutes. Reduce the heat to medium-low. Cover and cook until the lentils are tender, 20 to 25 minutes. Add the carrots, yam, tomato paste, and ginger. Stir well and cover. Continue cooking until all the vegetables are tender, 20 to 25 minutes.

Remove from the heat and discard the cilantro. Season with salt and pepper. Sprinkle with parsley and serve immediately.

FOUL MUDAMMAS

FAVA BEAN STEW WITH OLIVES (MOROCCO)

SERVES 4

IN MOROCCO, THIS DELICIOUS **TAGINE** IS CONSIDERED PEASANT FARE SINCE IT CONTAINS NO MEAT. IT USES TWO OF THE MOST READILY AVAILABLE INGREDIENTS IN THE COUNTRY, DRIED FAVA BEANS AND OLIVES. I FIND THAT THE TARTNESS OF THE OLIVES PERFECTLY COMPLEMENTS THE STRONG FLAVOR OF THE FAVA BEANS. **FOUL MUDAMMAS** ARE SMALL, SOMEWHAT ROUNDED, DARK-SKINNED FAVA BEANS, A STAPLE OF THE NORTH AFRICAN AND MIDDLE EASTERN DIET.

In a medium saucepan over medium-high heat, heat the olive oil. Add the garlic, tomatoes, cilantro, parsley, turmeric, pepper, and lemon juice. Cook, stirring, for 1 to 2 minutes. Reduce the heat to low and cook until the sauce thickens somewhat, 8 to 10 minutes. Lightly crush the olives with a fork and add them, along with the preserved lemon rind, to the tomato sauce. Cook 8 to 10 minutes and add the *foul mudammas.* Heat through for 4 to 5 minutes. Transfer to a serving dish. Garnish with cilantro or parsley.

2 tablespoons olive oil

3 garlic cloves, minced

3 tomatoes (1 pound), peeled, seeded
    (see page 24), and coarsely chopped

8 fresh cilantro sprigs, minced

8 fresh flat-leaf parsley sprigs, minced

1 teaspoon ground turmeric

½ teaspoon freshly ground black pepper

3 tablespoons fresh lemon juice

8 ounces (2 cups) green olives, pitted

2 teaspoons diced preserved lemon rind
    (page 15)

One 27-ounce can foul mudammas,
    drained

Minced fresh cilantro or parsley
    for garnish

KHALOTA

VEGETABLE MEDLEY (ALGERIA)

SERVES 4 TO 6

KHALOTA (PRONOUNCED "HĂLŌTA") IS A MEDLEY OF COOKED SEASONAL VEGETABLES SOMEWHAT LIKE RATATOUILLE. ZOULIKHA SENOUSSAOUI, WHO LEFT HER NATIVE ALGIERS FOR CASABLANCA WHEN SHE GOT MARRIED, REMEMBERS HER MOTHER MAKING **KHALOTA** OVER A CHARCOAL FIRE, LETTING THE DISH SIMMER UNTIL IT ATTAINED THE CONSISTENCY OF A THICK STEW. FAVA BEANS, WHICH ARE ALSO CALLED BROAD BEANS, ARE AMONG THE MOST WIDELY USED BEANS IN THE WORLD, YET THEY ARE SOMETIMES HARD TO FIND IN THE UNITED STATES. IF YOU ARE LUCKY ENOUGH TO HAVE A SOURCE OF FRESH FAVA BEANS, SELECT THEM WHEN THEY ARE SMALL, TENDER, AND CRISP.

2 tablespoons olive oil

1 small onion, finely diced

2½ teaspoons sweet paprika

6 garlic cloves, minced

15 fresh flat-leaf parsley sprigs, minced

3 carrots, peeled and diced

2 small potatoes (about ½ pound), peeled and diced

2 cups vegetable broth (page 23)

2 zucchini (about ½ pound), diced

1 medium globe eggplant (about ¾ pound), peeled and diced

8 ounces green beans, cut into 1-inch pieces

8 ounces fresh fava beans in their pods, strings removed, cut into 1-inch pieces, or one 10-ounce package frozen baby lima beans

Salt and freshly ground black pepper

¼ teaspoon cayenne

Minced fresh flat-leaf parsley for garnish

In a large saucepan over medium-high heat, heat the oil and cook the onion, stirring occasionally, until tender, 6 to 8 minutes. Add the paprika, three-fourths of the minced garlic cloves, and the parsley. Stir to blend. Add the carrots, potatoes, and broth. Cover and cook until the carrots lose their crispness, 8 to 10 minutes.

Reduce the heat to medium-low and add the zucchini, eggplant, green beans, and fava or lima beans. Cover and cook until all the vegetables are tender, 25 to 30 minutes. Season with salt, pepper, and cayenne to taste. Sprinkle with the minced parsley and remaining minced garlic and serve immediately.

chapter five

SIDE DISHES

SIDE DISHES

THE SEASON'S BOUNTY OF VEGETABLES INSPIRES NORTH AFRICAN COOKS TO CREATE A WEALTH OF DELICIOUS SIDE DISHES, FROM WINTER SQUASH WITH CARAMELIZED ONIONS to stuffed artichokes redolent of garlic, mint, *tabil,* and sweet paprika. Although they are called side dishes, they may also serve as the main course for a light meal, especially when accompanied with plenty of fresh, crusty bread, couscous, or rice.

A simple dish of potatoes and peas can be as satisfying as a multicourse meal. Just ask any of those who accompany me on the food tour I lead to Morocco every year. A picnic is always on the schedule. On one of those expeditions, the snow-capped Atlas Mountains provided a beautiful backdrop for an alfresco lunch in the middle of an orchard of flowering almond trees. A crowd of shy, yet curious Berber children gathered around our bus as soon as it came to a stop. Under their watchful gaze, Hadj Bouchta, our national guide, started charcoal fires in two or three *canouns* (braziers). He also unloaded several kilos of new potatoes and fresh peas that we had just purchased at the souk a half-hour earlier.

While Hadj and I cleaned and sliced the potatoes, other members of the group shelled the peas. Once the olive oil began to sizzle in the *tagine* dishes that had been set on the *canouns,* Hadj Bouchta quickly added the potatoes, along with judicious amounts of paprika, turmeric, salt, pepper, and some water, before capping each *tagine* with its distinctive conical lid. When the potatoes were tender, he added the peas and a handful of chopped cilantro. A few minutes later, he set the dishes in the middle of his hungry charges, who were seated on colorful blankets covering the ground. Cries of *Bravo!* rang out as he lifted each lid to reveal his aromatic creation. People helped themselves to the communal dishes using chunks of warm *kesra* bread (another one of our purchases at the souk) as their only utensil. This simple, yet delicious lunch set among such striking surroundings was not one that any of us would soon forget.

CASSOLITA

BAKED WINTER SQUASH WITH CARAMELIZED ONIONS (MOROCCO, ALGERIA)

SERVES 4

MY GREAT-GRANDMOTHER'S SEPHARDIC ANCESTORS FLED SPAIN AT THE TIME OF THE INQUISITION TO SETTLE IN ALGERIA. BECAUSE SHE SPOKE SPANISH, AS WELL AS FRENCH AND ARABIC, SHE REFERRED TO THIS DISH, ONE OF HER SPECIALTIES, AS **CASSOLITA**, NO DOUBT A WORD DERIVED FROM THE SPANISH **CAZUELA**, OR "LITTLE POT." THIS RECIPE REMAINS ONE OF THE MOST TREASURED IN OUR FAMILY. IT HAS BECOME A STANDARD SIDE DISH FOR OUR THANKSGIVING AND HOLIDAY MEALS. I LOVE THE SWEETNESS OF BUTTERNUT SQUASH IN THIS RECIPE, ALTHOUGH OTHER WINTER SQUASH VARIETIES SUCH AS ACORN, HUBBARD, OR SUGAR PUMPKIN WORK JUST AS WELL. SERVE **CASSOLITA** BY ITSELF, OR AS A TOPPING FOR COUSCOUS.

Preheat the oven to 375°F. Cut the neck of the squash into 1-inch-thick slices. Seed the bulbous end and cut it into chunks. Place the squash in an ovenproof dish. Add the ½ cup water and cover tightly. Bake until tender, 50 minutes to 1 hour. Drain off any remaining water.

Meanwhile, in a large skillet over medium heat, heat the oil and cook the onions, stirring occasionally, until almost caramelized, 10 to 12 minutes. If the mixture becomes too dry, add 1 or 2 tablespoons of water. Add the raisins, ¼ cup almonds, sugar, cinnamon, salt, and pepper. Cook, stirring, for 5 or 6 minutes. Spread the onion mixture evenly over the cooked squash. Bake until heated through, 10 to 15 minutes. To serve, sprinkle with a few slivered almonds.

2 pounds butternut squash, peeled

½ cup water, plus 1 or 2 tablespoons
water as needed

¼ cup vegetable oil

2 large onions, thinly sliced

½ cup black or golden raisins, plumped
in warm water and drained

¼ cup (1 ounce) slivered almonds, plus
more for garnish

¼ cup sugar

2 teaspoons ground cinnamon

Salt and freshly ground black pepper
to taste

ARTICHAUTS FARCIS

STUFFED ARTICHOKES (TUNISIA)

SERVES 4

ARTICHOKES ARE NATIVE TO THE MEDITERRANEAN BASIN, WHICH EXPLAINS THEIR POPULARITY IN THE LOCAL CUISINES. THE WORD ITSELF IS DERIVED FROM THE ARABIC WORD **AL HARSHOOF.** YOU CAN SERVE THESE STUFFED ARTICHOKES AS A MAIN COURSE FOR A LIGHT SUPPER, OR AS A SIDE DISH.

4 artichokes (about 2 pounds)

2 lemons

½ cup olive oil

1 onion, finely diced

4 to 6 slices plain white bread, crusts
removed, cubed

½ cup milk

4 garlic cloves

8 fresh flat-leaf parsley sprigs, minced

12 fresh mint leaves, chopped, or 3
teaspoons dried mint leaves, crushed

2 hard-cooked eggs, mashed

Grated zest of 1 lemon

2 teaspoons tabil *(page 22)*

Salt and freshly ground black pepper
to taste

½ teaspoon harissa (page 19)

2 teaspoons sweet paprika

½ cup vegetable broth (page 23)

Minced fresh flat-leaf parsley
for garnish

Remove the tough outer leaves from the artichokes. With kitchen shears or scissors, cut off the top of the artichokes crosswise to leave a 2-inch base. With a knife, cut a thin slice from the bottom of the artichokes to allow them to stand upright on a plate. In a large saucepan filled with boiling water, place the trimmed artichokes and half a lemon. Cook until the leaves are tender, 20 to 25 minutes. Drain and let cool. With a knife, remove the fuzzy chokes. Set the artichokes aside.

Preheat the oven to 375°F. In a small skillet over medium-high heat, heat 2 tablespoons of the oil and cook the onion, stirring occasionally, until tender, 6 to 8 minutes. In a medium bowl, soak the bread in the milk until it is soggy. In a blender or food processor, finely chop 2 garlic cloves, the parsley, mint, hard-cooked eggs, lemon zest, *tabil*, salt, pepper, and harissa. Mix with the soaked bread and the cooked onions.

Place the artichokes snugly inside an ovenproof baking dish. Fill the center of each artichoke with equal amounts of the stuffing. Mince the remaining 2 garlic cloves. In a small bowl, mix the juice from the remaining lemons with the paprika, the remaining 2 tablespoons olive oil, the minced garlic, and water. Pour this mixture over the artichokes. Cover tightly and bake until the leaves pull off easily, 30 to 35 minutes. Remove the cover, and place under the broiler for 3 to 4 minutes.

With a slotted spoon, transfer the artichokes to a serving platter and garnish with parsley. Serve hot with the sauce on the side.

K'RAA BEYDA

STUFFED ZUCCHINI IN EGG AND LEMON SAUCE (ALGERIA)

SERVES 4

IN OUJDA, A TOWN IN THE NORTHEASTERN CORNER OF MOROCCO, THE LOCAL CUISINE IS HEAVILY INFLUENCED BY IMMIGRANTS FROM NEARBY ALGERIA. THEY BROUGHT WITH THEM THIS DELIGHTFUL EGG AND LEMON SAUCE, WHICH THE PEOPLE OF THE AREA SERVE OVER STUFFED ZUCCHINI, A DISH THAT TRADITIONALLY USES A TOMATO BASE. WHAT A DELICIOUS EXAMPLE OF A CROSS-CULTURAL EXCHANGE!

5 zucchini (about 2 pounds)

Salt for sprinkling

4 tablespoons olive oil

1 onion, minced

½ red bell pepper, seeded, deribbed, and finely diced

½ cup cooked rice

½ teaspoon ground cinnamon

10 fresh flat-leaf parsley sprigs, minced

2 garlic cloves, minced

1 egg

½ teaspoon salt

⅛ teaspoon cayenne

1 teaspoon smen (page 18), (optional)

2 cups vegetable broth (page 23)

2 egg yolks

2 tablespoons fresh lemon juice

Minced fresh flat-leaf parsley for garnish

Peel the zucchini. Cut each one crosswise into 4 equal chunks. With a small spoon, scoop out the flesh, leaving a shell ¼-inch thick. Finely dice the reserved zucchini flesh and set aside. Place the shells snugly in an ovenproof dish. Sprinkle with a little salt and set aside in a bowl.

In a large skillet over medium-high heat, heat 2 tablespoons of the olive oil and cook the onion, stirring occasionally, until tender, 6 to 8 minutes. Add the diced zucchini and bell pepper and cook until tender. Set aside to cool.

Preheat the oven to 425°F. In a large bowl, combine the cooked vegetables, rice, cinnamon, parsley, garlic, egg, salt, cayenne, and optional *smen*. With a small spoon, carefully fill each zucchini cup with the mixture. Drizzle with the remaining 2 tablespoons olive oil. Add 1 cup of the broth. Cover tightly and bake for 30 to 35 minutes, until the zucchini is tender.

Reduce the heat to 350°F. Remove the zucchini from the oven. Drain off the pan juices into a small saucepan and add the remaining broth. Bring to a boil and reduce liquid to 1½ cups. In a small bowl, whisk the egg yolks with the lemon juice. Add the hot broth while whisking continuously. Pour the sauce over the zucchini and return the dish to the oven for 10 minutes to heat through. Sprinkle with parsley and serve.

AUBERGINES FARCIES

STUFFED EGGPLANTS (MOROCCO, ALGERIA, TUNISIA)

SERVES 4

IN NORTH AFRICA, BOTH GLOBE AND SLENDER EGGPLANTS ARE COMMONLY USED. THE VEGETABLE NOT ONLY MAKES A WONDERFUL EDIBLE RECEPTACLE, BUT ALSO STARS IN A HOST OF MEDITER-RANEAN DISHES, WHERE IT OFTEN SERVES AS SUBSTITUTE FOR MEAT. WHEN BUYING EGGPLANT, MAKE SURE THE FLESH IS SHINY AND FREE OF BLEMISHES. IT IS VERY PERISHABLE, AND CAN'T BE KEPT MORE THAN 1 OR 2 DAYS IN THE REFRIGERATOR.

Preheat the broiler. Trim the stems from the eggplants and cut the eggplants in half lengthwise. With a sharp knife, remove the flesh, leaving a ¼-inch-thick shell. Chop the eggplant flesh and set aside. Brush the inside of the shells with some of the olive oil and place them in an ovenproof dish. Broil them until they turn light brown, 4 or 5 minutes. Set aside.

Set the oven at 375°F. In a medium skillet over medium-high heat, heat the remainding olive oil and cook the onion, stirring occasionally, until tender, 6 to 8 minutes. Coarsely chop 2 of the tomatoes and add them to the onion. Add the chopped eggplant. Reduce the heat to medium. Cover and cook until the egg-plant is tender, 8 to 10 minutes.

Transfer the eggplant mixture to a bowl and mix it with the garlic, bread crumbs, cheese, parsley, basil, harissa, salt, and pepper. Fill the shells with this mixture. Slice the remaining tomatoes and arrange them on top of the stuffed eggplant. Drizzle with a little olive oil. Bake until lightly browned, 25 to 30 min-utes. Serve immediately.

2 globe eggplants (about 3 pounds)

3 tablespoons olive oil, plus olive oil for drizzling

1 onion, chopped

4 tomatoes (about 1⅓ pounds)

2 garlic cloves, minced

⅓ cup dried bread crumbs

⅓ cup (1½ ounces) freshly grated Parmesan cheese

12 fresh flat-leaf parsley sprigs, minced

8 fresh basil leaves, chopped

1 teaspoon harissa (page 19)

Salt and freshly ground black pepper to taste

HODRA MECHWYA

GRILLED VEGETABLE KABOBS WITH CHARMOULA MARINADE (MOROCCO)

SERVES 4

THE VERSATILE **CHARMOULA** SERVES AS A SAUCE AND A MARINADE IN A WIDE VARIETY OF MOROCCAN DISHES. ALTHOUGH TRADITIONALLY USED WITH SEAFOOD, IT IS ALSO MIXED WITH PUREED TOMATOES TO CREATE A DELICIOUS SAUCE FOR GREEN BEANS, FAVA BEANS, OR CARROTS. IN THIS DISH, IT IMPARTS A WONDERFUL FLAVOR TO FRESH VEGETABLES. SERVING LITTLE SAUCERS OF GROUND CUMIN ON THE SIDE IS THE TRADITION IN MOROCCO.

To make the *charmoula:* In a small bowl, combine all the ingredients and mix until well blended. Set aside.

Blanch the cauliflower in boiling water for 5 minutes. Drain and place in a large bowl, along with the zucchini, eggplant, bell pepper, fennel, and onions. Add the marinade and mix gently. Cover and refrigerate for 30 minutes or up to 4 hours, stirring occasionally.

Prepare a charcoal fire or preheat the broiler. Thread the marinated vegetables on metal skewers, reserving the marinade for basting. Grill or broil the vegetables, rotating the skewers carefully and basting the vegetables several times until lightly and evenly browned, 8 to 10 minutes. Serve hot, with cumin on the side.

Charmoula
½ cup olive oil
1 tablespoon ground cumin
2 tablespoons fresh lemon juice
½ teaspoon salt
¼ teaspoon freshly ground black pepper
1 tablespoon sweet paprika
½ teaspoon ground ginger
½ teaspoon dried marjoram
12 fresh cilantro sprigs, minced

Kabobs
1 small head cauliflower, separated into
    florets
2 zucchini, cut into 1-inch chunks
1 eggplant, peeled and cut into 1-inch
    chunks
1 red bell pepper, seeded, deribbed, and
    cut into 1-inch pieces
2 small fennel bulbs, quartered
12 pearl onions, peeled
Ground cumin for serving

chapter six

COUSCOUS, PASTA, AND RICE DISHES

COUSCOUS, PASTA, AND RICE DISHES

❋

COUSCOUS IS TO NORTH AFRICANS WHAT PASTA IS TO ITALIANS. IN **A WAYFARER IN MOROCCO**, ALYS LOWTH CAPTURED ITS IMPORTANCE AS A STAPLE:

> The dish par excellence is generally acknowledged to be *couscousoo* [*sic*] . . . an Arab variation of the Indian pilau—the Spanish pilaff—only with granulated flour, wheat, millet, or maize instead of rice; and with or without meat or chicken. The Arabs regard *couscousoo* literally with veneration. Like pilau, its excellence depends entirely upon the cook . . . there is literally no end to the variations. . . .

Indeed, as Dr. Naima Lakhal, a Moroccan economist, demonstrates in her dissertation, "La Production et la consommation du couscous au Maroc," not only is couscous still eaten several times a week in many Moroccan homes, it is also considered a sacred food by many North Africans, and is endowed with religious and even magical symbolism.

To me, couscous is food for the soul, as well as food for the body. When I was growing up, couscous was almost always synonymous with festive occasions. *"On fait un couscous!"* ("Let's make couscous!") my great-aunt Tita would announce. On relatively short notice, some twenty guests would appear, as if by magic—there always seemed to be enough food for twice that many—and gather around her massive dining room table to feast on a mountain of couscous. A tantalizing aroma of saffron-scented steam rose from the communal dish, which we eagerly attacked with large soup spoons. All of us, that is, except my grandfather Pépé, who preferred eating his couscous in the traditional manner. Using the three fingers of his right hand, he would break off a small piece of vegetable and deftly shape a small ball by mashing it with the steamed couscous. With a flick of his thumb, he propelled the ball into his mouth, as we all watched admiringly.

The origins of couscous have been traced to the nomadic Berbers of North Africa (although there are some food historians in Morocco who believe couscous already existed in Mesopotamia). They developed the method for making granules from cracked durum wheat, or semolina, as well as the process for steaming and drying the couscous. According to author Lucie Bolens in *La Cuisine andalouse: un art de vivre, XIe-XIIIe siècle*, primitive couscous pots have been found in tombs dating from the time of the Numidian king Massinissa (238–149 B.C.) It wasn't until the twelfth century, however, that formal recipes for couscous were mentioned in Andalusian texts. Whatever its origin, couscous, the staple of North African cuisine, is rapidly gaining in popularity in Europe and the United States. Although couscous is most commonly made from semolina, it is also sometimes made from barley grits, millet, or cornmeal.

Thomas Pellow, a sailor who spent twenty-three years as a captive among the Moors, gives us a wonderful description for the preparation of couscous in *The Adventures of Thomas Pellow, Of Penryn, Mariner: Three and Twenty Years in Captivity Among the Moors*:

. . . and for our dinner we seldom failed of the Moors' favorite dish cuscassoo [*sic*] . . . for it is actually very good, grateful and nourishing, and is prepared after the following manner: first they put fine flour into a large wooden bowl, then they pour thereon a small quantity of water, and keep continually shaking the bowl til the water is drank up; then they pour on some more, and so continue to shake the bowl, till all the flour is come to small pellets of about the bigness of Nutmegs [*sic*] . . . then they are put out of the bowl into another utensil like a cullender [*sic*] . . .

After describing the steaming process, Pellow concludes: "This, I say, is excellent eating."

Although modern production techniques are now employed to make couscous, many North African housewives still prefer to "roll their own." The semolina is placed in a large earthenware platter, sprinkled with lightly salted water and flour, and adroitly raked with open fingers until all the water is absorbed. It is then "rolled," using a rhythmic, circular motion, until tiny granules form. These granules of varying sizes are separated from one another using a series of sieves. The finest granules, called *s'ffa*, should be "the size of ants' heads," according to the thirteenth-century jurist Ibn Razin Al-Tujibi of Murcia. In the United States, medium-grade couscous is the kind most widely available commercially.

To steam couscous in the traditional manner, you will need a *keskes,* or as the French call it, a *couscoussier,* which is a large soup pot topped with a tight-fitting colander. The pot and the colander are sealed with a thin strip of damp cloth so that all the steam from the simmering broth is forced into the couscous, causing it to swell. After 8 to 10 minutes of steaming, the couscous is transferred to a large platter and mixed with butter, *smen* (page 18), broth, or a little olive oil to give it additional flavor. Some North African cooks steam their couscous as many as seven times! Usually, however, the steaming process is repeated two or three times, 8 to 10 minutes each, to obtain a light and fluffy couscous that is then mixed with the flavoring ingredients. Barley grits can also be steamed in the same manner. You can substitute a large soup pot with a tight-fitting sieve lined with cheesecloth or muslin, if necessary.

This lengthy steaming process isn't required when using the instant couscous that is readily available in the pasta section of most American supermarkets, natural foods stores, or specialty markets. Instant couscous has been pre-steamed, and will plump up to four times its original size simply by being mixed with the required amount of hot liquid. For a more authentic flavor and consistency, however, you can also steam instant couscous over boiling broth in the traditional manner. To do so, place the required amount of couscous in a bowl, and barely cover it with water. Let it stand for 1 or 2 minutes until the water is absorbed. (Do not add excess water or the couscous will turn into a lumpy mass.) Place the couscous in the colander or couscoussier. Line it with muslin or cheesecloth, although that isn't mandatory since the boiling broth from the pot will prevent the couscous from falling through. Steam the couscous for 4 to 5 minutes, uncovered, watching carefully so that it doesn't turn lumpy. Transfer it to a bowl, fluff it with a fork, and mix with 1 tablespoon of butter or olive oil, and serve immediately.

Moroccans and Algerians serve couscous immediately before the dessert course, mounded on a large platter. They decorate its "face" with the meat and/or vegetables that have been simmering in the broth. Harissa, the Tunisian hot sauce popular throughout the Maghreb, is served on the side with extra broth. Tunisians, whose palates are more accustomed to the piquant harissa, like to mix the couscous with a liberal dose of the fiery sauce before bringing it to the table.

COUSCOUS AUX FENOUILS MEHERZIA

MEHERZIA'S COUSCOUS WITH FENNEL (TUNISIA)

SERVES 6

MEHERZIA JAZIRI AND HER SON MONCEF TAUGHT ME HOW TO MAKE THIS DELIGHTFUL AND UN-USUAL COUSCOUS, WHICH USES BOTH FENNEL FRONDS AND BULBS. SINCE MOST FOOD STORES CUT OFF THE FRONDS AND DISPLAY ONLY THE BULBS, CALL THE PRODUCE DEPARTMENT AT YOUR LOCAL SUPERMARKET AHEAD OF TIME TO HAVE THE FRONDS SAVED FOR YOU. ADD THE FENNEL FRONDS TO THE COUSCOUS BEFORE STEAMING. IN TUNISIA, COUSCOUS IS USUALLY SERVED WITH A MIXTURE OF PICKLED VEGETABLES CALLED **TORCHI**.

Cut off the stalks from the fennel bulbs. Remove the feathery fronds from the tough stalks, discarding the stalks. Finely chop all the fronds and set aside. You should have about 6 to 8 loosely packed cups. Quarter the fennel bulbs and set aside.

In a large saucepan over medium-high heat, heat the olive oil and cook the onions and the garlic, stirring occasionally, until tender, 6 to 8 minutes. In a small bowl, dilute the tomato paste and 2 teaspoons harissa in 1 cup of the water. Add this to the saucepan along with the remaining 6 cups water, chilies, *tabil*, and salt. Bring to a rolling boil and add the quartered fennel bulbs. Lower the heat to medium. Cover and cook until the fennel is just tender, 12 to 15 minutes. With a slotted spoon, transfer the fennel, chilies, and onions to a bowl. Cover and keep warm. Continue simmering the broth.

In another large saucepan, place 2¼ cups of the simmering broth and the butter. Bring to a boil and add all but 2 tablespoons of the fennel fronds. Cook for 2 or 3 minutes. Remove from the heat and stir in the couscous. Cover and let stand for 5 minutes. Transfer the couscous to a large bowl. Fluff it with a fork to break up any lumps. Add the optional *smen* and mix well.

Heap the couscous on a large platter. Arrange the fennel bulbs and the onions over the couscous. Ring the platter with the chilies. Sprinkle the dish lightly and evenly with 1 cup of the broth. Garnish with the reserved chopped fennel fronds. Serve with extra harissa on the side.

4 fennel bulbs (about 1 pound each), with fronds, plus 1 pound of fronds

3 tablespoons olive oil

2 onions, quartered

4 garlic cloves, minced

3 tablespoons tomato paste

2 teaspoons harissa (page 19), plus extra for serving

7 cups water

4 Anaheim chilies, halved lengthwise, seeded, and deribbed

1 tablespoon tabil (page 22)

2 teaspoons salt

2 tablespoons unsalted butter

2 cups (14 ounces) instant couscous

1 tablespoon smen (page 18), (optional)

COUSCOUS MESFOUF

COUSCOUS WITH DRIED FRUIT (MOROCCO, ALGERIA, TUNISIA)

SERVES 6 TO 8

STEAMED COUSCOUS MIXED WITH DRIED FRUIT AND NUTS AND SPRINKLED WITH SUGAR AND CINNA-MON IS SERVED DURING SPECIAL CELEBRATIONS IN THE MAGHREB. **COUSCOUS MESFOUF** (A LOOSE TRANSLATION OF **MESFOUF** IS "CONCEALED") USUALLY PRECEDES DESSERT, AND IS ACCOMPANIED WITH A COOL GLASS OF BUTTERMILK. IN NORTH AFRICA, IT IS MADE WITH **S'FFA**, A GRADE OF COUSCOUS AS FINE AS CORNMEAL, WHICH IS, I'M SORRY TO SAY, NOT YET AVAILABLE COMMERCIALLY IN THIS COUNTRY.

2½ cups vegetable broth (page 23)

4 tablespoons unsalted butter

6 Spanish saffron threads, crushed

⅓ cup (2 ounces) chopped dried apricots

⅓ cup (2 ounces) chopped dates

⅓ cup (2 ounces) seedless raisins

2 cups (14 ounces) instant couscous

2 teaspoons ground cinnamon

3 tablespoons granulated sugar

1 tablespoon smen (page 18)

½ cup (2 ounces) slivered almonds, toasted (page 24)

Sifted confectioner's sugar and ground cinnamon for garnish

In a large saucepan, bring 2 cups of the broth to a low boil. Add the butter, saffron, apricots, dates, and raisins. Cook until the raisins plump, 2 to 3 minutes. Remove from the heat and add the couscous. Stir to blend. Cover and let stand for 5 minutes.

Transfer the couscous to a bowl. Fluff it with a fork to break up any lumps. Add the cinnamon, sugar, and smen to the couscous and mix thoroughly. Shape the couscous into a conical mound on a large serving platter. Heat the remaining broth and sprinkle it over the couscous. Holding a little sugar or cinnamon between your thumb and forefinger, create thin stripes down the sides of the mound of couscous, from the peak to the base, alternating lines of slivered almonds, confectioners' sugar, and ground cinnamon to look like the ribs of a half-opened umbrella. Serve hot.

COUSCOUS BEIDAOUI

COUSCOUS CASABLANCA STYLE (MOROCCO)

SERVES 6

THIS IS THE COUSCOUS I WAS RAISED ON. IT IS A SPECIALTY FROM MY HOMETOWN OF CASABLANCA, OR DAR BEIDA, AS IT IS KNOWN IN ARABIC. ACCORDING TO TRADITION, AT LEAST SEVEN DIFFERENT SEASONAL VEGETABLES MUST BE SIMMERED IN THE AROMATIC SAFFRON AND GINGER-SCENTED BROTH TO QUALIFY IT AS A COUSCOUS **BEIDAOUI**. THIS IS WONDERFUL SERVED WITH HARISSA.

In a large soup pot over medium heat, combine the water, saffron, ginger, parsley, cilantro, tomatoes, celery, squash, carrots, and turnips. Cover and cook until the vegetables are crisp-tender, 15 to 20 minutes. Add the zucchini and the lima beans and cook until tender, 6 to 8 minutes. Reduce the heat to a simmer. Add the garbanzo beans. Season with salt and pepper. Discard the parsley and the cilantro.

In a large saucepan, combine 2 cups of broth from the soup pot and the butter. Bring to a low boil. Remove from the heat and add the couscous. Stir to blend. Cover and let stand for 5 minutes. Transfer the couscous to a large bowl. Fluff it with a fork to break up any lumps. Add the optional *smen* and mix well.

Make a bed of couscous on a large serving platter. With a slotted spoon, remove the vegetables from the broth, arranging them over and around the couscous. Sprinkle with 1 cup of the hot broth and garnish with the raisins. Serve immediately with extra hot broth and harissa (page 19), if using, on the side.

6 cups water

8 Spanish saffron threads, crushed

1 teaspoon ground ginger

15 fresh flat-leaf parsley sprigs, tied
    with cotton string

20 fresh cilantro sprigs, tied with cotton
    string

2 tomatoes (12 ounces), cut into 1-inch
    cubes

4 celery stalks, cut into 1-inch pieces

1 pound butternut squash, peeled, seeded,
    and cut into 2-inch chunks

4 carrots, peeled and cut into sticks 3
    inches long

2 small turnips, peeled and quartered

2 zucchini, scraped and cut into sticks 3
    inches long

1 10-ounce package frozen baby lima beans

1 cup canned garbanzo beans, drained

Salt and freshly ground black pepper to taste

2 tablespoons unsalted butter

2 cups (14 ounces) instant couscous

1 tablespoon smen (page 18), (optional)

½ cup raisins, plumped

COUSCOUS BELBOULA

BARLEY GRIT COUSCOUS (MOROCCO, ALGERIA, TUNISIA)

SERVES 4

IN BARLEY-PRODUCING REGIONS OF NORTH AFRICA, A SPECIAL COUNTRY-STYLE COUSCOUS IS MADE WITH BARLEY GRITS, OR **BELBOULA**. THE TEXTURE IS SOMEWHAT COARSER THAN THAT OF COUSCOUS. BARLEY GRITS ARE AVAILABLE IN THE CEREAL SECTION OF MOST NATURAL FOODS STORES. THEY ARE COOKED IN THE SAME WAY AS INSTANT COUSCOUS.

2 tablespoons olive oil

1 onion, sliced

2 large tomatoes, quartered

24 fresh cilantro sprigs, tied with cotton string

4 cups vegetable broth (page 23)

1 teaspoon ground turmeric

1 teaspoon freshly ground black pepper

½ teaspoon ground cinnamon

3 carrots, peeled and cut into sticks

2 rutabagas, cut into 1-inch cubes

1 globe eggplant, peeled and cut into large chunks

2 zucchini, cut into ½-inch-thick sticks

Salt to taste

2 tablespoons unsalted butter

1 cup barley grits

1 tablespoon smen (page 18) or olive oil

Preheat the oven to 200°F. In a large soup pot over medium-high heat, heat the oil and cook the onion, stirring occasionally, until tender, 6 to 8 minutes. Add the tomatoes, cilantro, broth, turmeric, pepper, and cinnamon. Cover and bring to a rolling boil. Add the carrots and rutabagas and lower the heat to medium. Cover and cook until the vegetables are crisp-tender, 15 to 20 minutes.

Add the eggplant and zucchini and cook until tender, 10 to 12 minutes. To prevent the vegetables from overcooking, with a slotted spoon, transfer them to an ovenproof dish and keep them warm in the oven until ready to serve. Keep the broth simmering in the pot. Discard the cilantro and season with salt.

In a medium saucepan, place 1 cup of the broth and 2 tablespoons of butter, and bring to a low boil. Remove from the heat and add the barley grits. Stir to blend. Cover and let stand for 5 minutes. Transfer to a large bowl. Fluff the barley grits with a fork to break up any lumps. Sprinkle lightly with ½ cup of the broth to moisten. Add the *smen* or olive oil and mix well.

Arrange the barley grits around the perimeter of a serving platter. Place the vegetables in the center. Serve with some of the remaining broth on the side.

COUSCOUS KABYLE

COUSCOUS FROM THE KABYLIE REGION (ALGERIA)

SERVES 4

THE KABYLIE, THE MOUNTAINOUS AREA EAST OF ALGIERS, IS THE DOMAIN OF THE KABYLE BERBERS. IT IS ALSO THE COUNTRY'S RICHEST AGRICULTURAL REGION. ACCORDING TO NACIRA BABA-AHMED, A FRIEND WHO WAS BORN IN TLEMCEN, THIS LOVELY DISH, ALSO CALLED A SAVORY **MESFOUF** (MEANING "CONCEALED"), IS TYPICAL OF KABYLE CUISINE. "MY AMERICAN FRIENDS SAY THEY LIKE IT BECAUSE IT'S SO LIGHT YET FULL OF FLAVOR," SHE SAYS. THE COUSCOUS IS MIXED WITH COLORFUL BITS OF STEAMED VEGETABLES, WHICH VARY ACCORDING TO THE SEASON. NASSIRA MAKES THIS WITH THE WHOLE-WHEAT COUSCOUS AVAILABLE IN MANY AMERICAN SUPERMARKETS. SINCE OLIVE OIL GIVES THE COUSCOUS ITS FLAVOR, USE THE FRUITIEST EXTRA-VIRGIN OIL YOU CAN FIND. USE COUSCOUS KABYLE AS A SIDE DISH, OR SERVE IT THE WAY THE ALGERIANS DO, AS AN ENTREE, ACCOMPANIED WITH A GLASS OF BUTTERMILK.

Steam the green beans, carrots, lima beans, and baby peas over boiling water until crisp-tender, 6 to 8 minutes. Remove from the heat and keep warm.

In a large saucepan, bring the broth to a boil. Remove from the heat and add the couscous. Stir to blend. Cover and let stand for 6 to 8 minutes. Transfer the couscous to a large bowl. Fluff it with a fork to break up any lumps. Add the ¼ cup olive oil and mix well. Mix the couscous with the vegetables. Season with salt.

Mound the couscous on a serving platter and sprinkle with the parsley. Serve immediately. Drizzle a little extra olive oil over each serving.

4 ounces green beans, cut into small dice

2 carrots, peeled and finely diced

One 10-ounce package frozen baby lima beans

1 cup frozen baby peas

2¼ cups vegetable broth (page 23)

2 cups (14 ounces) whole-wheat couscous

¼ cup extra-virgin olive oil, plus more for drizzling

Salt to taste

6 fresh flat-leaf parsley sprigs, minced

SPAGHETTI KERKENNAISE

SPAGHETTI WITH FRESH TOMATO AND CAPER SAUCE (TUNISIA)

SERVES 4

THE SAUCE GETS ITS NAME FROM THE ISLANDS OF KERKENNAH JUST OFF THE CENTRAL COAST OF TUNISIA. CHEZ ACHOUR, ONE OF THE MOST POPULAR RESTAURANTS IN THE SEASIDE RESORT TOWN OF HAMMAMET, SERVES IT AS A TOPPING FOR SEAFOOD. IN THIS RECIPE, HOWEVER, I USE **SAUCE KERKENNAISE** AS A TOPPING FOR PASTA. IT IS ALSO DELICIOUS WHEN SERVED AS A DIP WITH CRISP **DOIGTS DE FATMA** (PAGE 33).

Preheat the broiler. Place the tomatoes on a lightly oiled baking sheet, and broil about 3 inches from the heat source, until the skins are evenly blackened. Set aside to cool. Broil the unpeeled garlic cloves until lightly browned on both sides, 5 to 6 minutes. Set aside to cool.

When the tomatoes are cool enough to handle, peel, seed, and finely dice them. Place them in a colander to drain for 30 minutes. Squeeze the tender garlic cloves out of their skins and mash them coarsely with a fork. Set aside.

Transfer the tomatoes to a serving bowl. Stir in the garlic, capers, caper juice, half of the parsley, 1 tablespoon of the olive oil, salt, pepper, harissa, and optional jalapeño.

In a large saucepan, bring 2 quarts of lightly salted water to a boil. Cook the pasta until al dente according to package directions, or about 6 to 8 minutes for capellini and 8 to 10 minutes for spaghetti. Drain well and transfer to a serving bowl. Toss with the remaining 1 tablespoon olive oil. To serve, mound the pasta in a shallow bowl, and top with the tomato and caper sauce. Garnish with the remaining parsley.

Sauce Kerkennaise

3 large tomatoes

8 unpeeled garlic cloves

2 tablespoons capers, drained

2 teaspoons caper juice

15 fresh flat-leaf parsley sprigs, minced

2 tablespoons olive oil

*Salt and freshly ground black pepper
    to taste*

1 tablespoon harissa (page 19)

*1 jalapeño chili, seeded, deribbed, and
    minced (optional)*

*12 ounces spaghetti or dried capellini
    (angel hair) pasta*

COUSCOUS T'FAYA

COUSCOUS WITH CARAMELIZED ONIONS AND RAISINS (MOROCCO, ALGERIA, TUNISIA)

SERVES 4

A PLATTER OF COUSCOUS OFTEN TAKES ON A SYMBOLIC MEANING IN NORTH AFRICA. THIS DISH, FOR EXAMPLE, IS TRADITIONALLY SERVED AT WEDDING **DIFFAS** (BANQUETS). WITH ITS SWEET TOPPING OF CARAMELIZED ONIONS AND RAISINS, **COUSCOUS T'FAYA** SYMBOLIZES THE WISH FOR A SWEET LIFE FOR THE NEWLY WEDDED COUPLE.

4 tablespoons unsalted butter

4 large onions, very thinly sliced

1 teaspoon ground cinnamon

½ teaspoon ground ginger

2 teaspoons sugar

½ cup raisins

Salt and freshly ground black pepper
to taste

2¼ cups vegetable broth (page 23)

6 Spanish saffron threads, crushed

2 cups (14 ounces) instant couscous

3 hard-cooked eggs, halved

¼ cup sliced almonds, toasted
(see page 24)

In a large skillet over medium heat, melt 2 tablespoons of the butter and cook the onions, stirring occasionally, until tender, 6 to 8 minutes. Add the cinnamon, ginger, sugar, raisins, salt, and pepper. Reduce heat to low. Cover and cook, stirring occasionally, until the onions acquire a nice caramel color, 25 to 30 minutes. Set aside and keep warm.

In a large saucepan, combine the broth, saffron, and the remaining 2 tablespoons butter. Bring to a low boil. Remove from heat and add the couscous. Stir to blend. Cover and let stand for 5 minutes. Transfer the couscous to a large bowl. Fluff it with a fork to break up any lumps.

Mound the couscous on a serving platter. Top it with the onion mixture. Set the egg halves, yolk-side down, around the base of the couscous. Garnish with toasted almonds.

TBIKHA AUX LÉGUMES

GREEN BEANS AND CARROTS WITH RICE (ALGERIA)

SERVES 6

TBIKHA (PRONOUNCED "TBĒ-HĂ"), A SPICY VEGETABLE MEDLEY, IS OFTEN MADE WITH FRESH YOUNG FAVA BEANS, PODS INCLUDED. SINCE THESE ARE SOMETIMES DIFFICULT TO FIND IN THE UNITED STATES, I HAVE SUBSTITUTED GREEN BEANS. THE COOKING TIME MIGHT SEEM A LITTLE LONG TO THOSE ACCUSTOMED TO EATING THEIR VEGETABLES AL DENTE, BUT THESE BEANS ARE NOT SUPPOSED TO BE CRISP.

In a heavy saucepan over medium-high heat, heat the olive oil. Cook the onion, stirring occasionally, until tender, 6 to 8 minutes. Add the paprika and garlic and stir until the onion is well coated. Add the tomatoes and cook until they are tender, 3 to 4 minutes. Add the carrots, green beans, water, and half of the cilantro. Cover and reduce heat to low. Cook until the carrots are just tender, 8 to 10 minutes.

Add the peas, cayenne, and rice. Continue cooking, covered, until the rice is tender, 20 to 25 minutes. Salt to taste and sprinkle with the remaining cilantro. Serve immediately.

3 tablespoons olive oil

1 onion, finely diced

1½ teaspoons sweet paprika

4 garlic cloves, minced

3 tomatoes (1 pound), peeled, seeded (page 24), and coarsely chopped

2 carrots, peeled and finely diced

1 pound green beans, cut in half crosswise

1 cup water

24 fresh cilantro sprigs, minced

1 cup frozen baby peas

⅛ teaspoon cayenne

⅓ cup long-grain rice

Salt to taste

chapter seven

SAVORY PASTRIES, BREADS, AND SANDWICHES

SAVORY PASTRIES, BREADS, AND SANDWICHES

SAVORY PASTRIES

FROM **BASTILA** (PAGE 127) TO **BREIKS** (PAGE 124) AND **BOUREKS** (PAGE 128), NORTH AFRICAN COOKS HAVE ELEVATED THE CREATION OF SAVORY PASTRIES TO A DELECTABLE ART FORM. Indeed, Moroccan *bastila,* proof of the culinary genius of the Andalusian Arabs, is cited as one of the highlights of Moroccan cuisine by chefs the world over. This golden and flaky phyllo "pie" usually encloses an exquisitely seasoned filling of shredded fowl cooked in a sauce redolent with saffron, cinnamon, parsley, and cilantro. The meatless version in this chapter contains a mixture of crushed nuts and scrambled eggs blended with fresh herbs and some of these exotic spices.

Light and crispy *breiks* are the delicious trademark of Tunisian cuisine. Each cook prides herself on making the perfect egg *breik,* which must retain a golden crispiness while the yolk inside remains runny enough to ooze from the turnover as you bite into it. The contents of a *breik* can also vary, from a spicy mixture of vegetables, onions, and herbs, to a blend of potatoes and capers.

Traditionally, *bastila, breiks,* and Algerian *boureks* are made with a paper-thin pastry dough made from wheat flour. It somewhat resembles Greek phyllo, yet in texture and workability it is more closely akin to Chinese egg roll skins. In Morocco, the word for this dough is *ouarka,* which in Arabic means "leaf"; in Tunisia it is called *malsouka,* and in Algeria, *feuilles de dioul.* Both phyllo and egg roll skins are good substitutes.

Making this dough requires a dexterity obtained from years of practice. Throughout North Africa, there are professional cooks who specialize in this one food. To make it, a wad of tender, moist dough is rhythmically dabbed on the bottom of a large copper pan that has been set upside down over a charcoal fire. This is done until the whole surface of the pan is covered with a thin film of overlapping circles of cooked dough as light and translucent as a butterfly's wing. Many modern-day housewives in the Maghreb, however, choose to purchase the ready-made sheets of *ouarka, malsouka,* or *dioul* available at their local market.

TARTE À LA FRITA

SWEET PEPPER TART (ALGERIA)

MAKES ONE 8-INCH TART; SERVES 4

AMONG THE DELICIOUS DISHES THAT CONTRIBUTED TO MY GREAT-GRANDMOTHER'S REPUTATION AS A FINE COOK WAS THIS ALGERIAN **FRITA**, A BLEND OF BELL PEPPERS AND TOMATOES SIMMERED TO AN ALMOST JAMLIKE CONSISTENCY, SIMILAR TO TUNISIAN **CHAKCHOUKA**. FREQUENTLY, SHE WOULD USE IT AS A FILLING FOR A TART. THE FOLLOWING RECIPE IS USUALLY SERVED FOR A LIGHT DINNER OR A FIRST COURSE. I LIKE TO USE A MIXTURE OF GREEN AND RED PEPPERS TO GIVE THE TART ADDED COLOR.

In a medium bowl, mix the flour with the salt. Using a pastry blender or 2 knives, cut in the shortening until the mixture resembles coarse crumbs. Stir the water and 1 lightly beaten egg gradually until the pastry is just moist enough to hold together. Do not overwork it or the crust will be tough. Separate the dough into 2 equal balls. Cover with plastic wrap and refrigerate for 30 minutes.

Preheat the broiler. Place the peppers on a lightly oiled baking sheet and broil about 3 inches from the heat source, turning carefully with tongs, until the skins are evenly charred. Place them in a paper or plastic bag and close it. Reduce the heat to 425°F. When the peppers are cool, peel and seed them. Cut the peppers into thin strips and set aside in a colander to drain.

In a large skillet over medium heat, heat the olive oil. Add the tomatoes, garlic, tomato paste, cumin, and olives. Cook, uncovered, until most of the liquid from the tomatoes evaporates. Add the peppers. Season with the salt, pepper, and cayenne. Cook, stirring occasionally, until the *frita* is reduced to an almost jamlike consistency, 10 to 15 minutes. Remove from the heat and let cool.

Lightly grease an 8-inch pie pan. On a floured surface, carefully roll out the dough into two 10-inch circles. Line the bottom of the pan with one circle of dough and fill it with *frita*. Cover with the second circle of dough. Trim off the excess and crimp the edges to seal. With a sharp knife, make 4 slits in the top crust. Brush lightly with the second beaten egg. Bake in a preheated oven for 20 minutes. Reduce the heat to 350°F and bake until the crust is golden, 15 to 20 minutes. Serve immediately.

2 cups unbleached all-purpose flour

½ teaspoon salt

10 tablespoons vegetable shortening

¼ cup cold water

2 eggs

4 bell peppers

2 tablespoons olive oil

4 tomatoes (1⅓ pounds), peeled, seeded (page 24), and coarsely diced

2 garlic cloves, minced

2 tablespoons tomato paste

1 teaspoon ground cumin

12 Kalamata or niçoise olives, pitted and sliced

Salt and freshly ground black pepper to taste

⅛ teaspoon cayenne

EGG BREIKS

TUNISIAN EGG TURNOVERS

MAKES 4 **BREIKS**; SERVES 4 AS A FIRST COURSE, 2 AS AN ENTREE

T HIS TUNISIAN SPECIALTY HAS BECOME POPULAR THROUGHOUT NORTH AFRICA AS WELL AS IN FRANCE, THANKS TO THE MIGRATION OF THE PIEDS-NOIRS. **BREIKS** ENFOLD AN ARRAY OF FILLINGS FROM EGG TO TUNA FISH TO CUBES OF CHEESE MIXED WITH CHOPPED HERBS. **BREIKS** MUST BE ASSEMBLED WHEN GUESTS ARE ALREADY SEATED AT THE TABLE SO THAT THE CRISP PASTRY CAN BE EATEN **IMMEDI- ATELY** AFTER IT IS FRIED. I LIKE TO USE EGG ROLL SKINS BECAUSE THEY ARE EASIER TO WORK WITH AND SOMEWHAT CRISPER THAN PHYLLO DOUGH (SEE NOTE BELOW).

4 eggs

32 fresh flat-leaf parsley sprigs, minced

8 fresh cilantro sprigs, minced

4 teaspoons finely chopped onion

Salt and freshly ground black pepper
*   to taste*

Four 7-inch-square Chinese egg roll
*   skins*

Vegetable oil for frying

1 teaspoon harissa (page 19), (optional)

Lemon wedges for garnish

Make 1 *breik* at a time. Break each egg into a separate small bowl. Set aside. In a medium bowl, mix the parsley, cilantro, onion, salt, and pepper. Set aside. Unwrap the egg roll skins. Line a plate or a tray with paper towels. Into a medium skillet, pour oil to a depth of ½ inch. Heat it over medium-high heat to 325°F, or until a little piece of egg roll skin sizzles instantly when added. Place half of 1 egg roll skin in the oil, letting the other half hang over the side of the pan. Carefully pour 1 of the eggs onto the frying egg roll skin. Sprinkle with one-fourth of the premixed herbs and spices. Add harissa, if using. With a spatula, gently close the *breik* to form a large rectangle. Press along the edges to seal them. Cook until golden, 1 to 2 minutes on each side. (The yolk should remain runny.) Drain well on paper towels. Serve *immediately* with lemon wedges.

N O T E : You can also use phyllo to make *breiks.* If so, use a double layer and proceed as directed in the recipe.

POTATO BREIKS WITH OLIVES AND CAPERS

TUNISIAN POTATO TURNOVERS (TUNISIA)

MAKES 14 **BREIKS**; SERVES 14 AS A FIRST COURSE, 7 AS AN ENTREE

I SPENT A SUMMER MANY YEARS AGO WITH A TUNISIAN FAMILY WHILE STUDYING AT THE BOURGUIBA SCHOOL IN TUNIS. ON MANY NIGHTS MY HOSTESS SERVED THESE DELIGHTFUL TURNOVERS AS THE MAIN COURSE FOR A LIGHT SUPPER. SHE WOULD SIMPLY ACCOMPANY THEM WITH ONE OR TWO VEGETABLE SALADS, SUCH AS **OMMOK HOURIA** (PAGE 56), OR WITH A BOWL OF HEARTY **CHORBA** (PAGE 48).

Place the potatoes in a large saucepan filled with cold water to cover. Add the salt and cook, partially covered, for 25 to 30 minutes, or until a knife pierces a potato easily. Drain, reserving 1 cup of the cooking liquid, and let the potatoes cool. Peel them and return them to the pot. Using a masher or a ricer, mash the potatoes until smooth. Add enough of the reserved cooking liquid to obtain a thick puree. Stir in the olive oil, onion, capers, olives, parsley, pepper flakes, and black pepper until well blended.

Line a baking sheet with paper towels. Set aside. Separate the egg roll skins and place them on a clean surface. Place ¼ cup of the potato mixture in the center of each egg roll skin. Fold over to make a triangular-shaped turnover. Seal the edges with water.

Into a medium skillet, pour oil to a depth of ½ inch. Heat it over medium heat to 325°F, or until a piece of egg roll skin sizzles slowly when added. (If the oil is too hot, the dough will cook before the filling is heated through.) Carefully set one *breik* at a time in the oil. Fry until golden brown, 2 to 3 minutes on each side. Drain well on paper towels. Serve *immediately* with lemon wedges. Repeat to cook the remaining turnovers.

2½ pounds russet potatoes, scrubbed and quartered

1 teaspoon salt

¼ cup olive oil

½ small onion, finely diced

2 tablespoons capers, drained

10 green or black olives, pitted and chopped

10 fresh flat-leaf parsley sprigs, minced

1 teaspoon red pepper flakes

½ teaspoon freshly ground black pepper

Fourteen 7-inch-square Chinese egg roll skins

Vegetable oil for frying

Lemon wedges for garnish

CASHEW BASTILA

CASHEW PHYLLO PIE (MOROCCO)

SERVES 4

THIS IS AN ADAPTATION OF **BASTILA**, THE FAMOUS FLAKY PHYLLO PASTRY OF MOROCCO. SHREDDED SQUAB OR, IN MORE RECENT YEARS, CHICKEN IS TRADITIONALLY USED IN THIS DISH. MOROCCANS OF MORE MODEST MEANS USE GROUND PEANUTS INSTEAD OF THE ALMONDS USUALLY CALLED FOR IN THIS DISH. IN THIS MEATLESS VARIATION, I USE CASHEWS INSTEAD. I THINK YOU'LL AGREE THAT THE RESULT IS DELICIOUS AND QUITE UNUSUAL.

Preheat the oven to 400°F. In a medium skillet, heat 2 tablespoons of the butter and cook the green onions over medium heat, stirring occasionally, until tender, 4 to 5 minutes. In a medium bowl, beat the eggs with the cinnamon, paprika, salt, and pepper. Add the egg mixture to the onions and scramble until the eggs are fairly dry. With a fork, stir in the parsley, cilantro, and cashews. Set aside to cool.

Melt the remaining 6 tablespoons butter. Place the phyllo sheets on a damp towel. Using a bowl about 11 inches in diameter as a template, cut through the 8 layers of phyllo. Place 4 rounds of phyllo, brushing each one with melted butter, so that they cover the bottom and overlap the sides of a well-greased 8-inch pie pan. Spread the egg mixture evenly over the phyllo. Fold the outside edges of phyllo over the filling. Cover with the 4 remaining sheets of phyllo, buttering each one as it is placed. Carefully fold the top sheets under the pie as you would a bedsheet. Generously brush the top with butter. Bake the *bastila* until golden brown, 20 to 25 minutes. Serve immediately.

8 tablespoons (1 stick) unsalted butter

8 green onions with tops, chopped

6 eggs

1 teaspoon ground cinnamon

1 teaspoon sweet paprika

½ teaspoon salt

¼ teaspoon freshly ground black pepper

12 fresh flat-leaf parsley sprigs, minced

10 fresh cilantro sprigs, minced

1 cup (about 7 ounces) cashew pieces, finely chopped

8 phyllo sheets

BOUREKS FELFEL

SWEET PEPPER TURNOVERS (ALGERIA)

MAKES SIXTEEN 3-BY-4-INCH **BOUREKS**; SERVES 16 AS AN APPETIZER, 8 AS AN ENTREE

THESE ALGERIAN **BOUREKS** ARE FRIED PASTRIES MADE OF **DIOUL**, A PAPER-THIN DOUGH SIMILAR TO PHYLLO, FILLED WITH A SAVORY MIXTURE OF VEGETABLES, HERBS, AND SPICES. LIKE OTHER PHYLLO PASTRIES, THEY MUST BE SERVED **IMMEDIATELY** AFTER FRYING.

2 red bell peppers

2 green bell peppers

2 tablespoons olive oil

1 onion, finely chopped

2 garlic cloves, minced

1 teaspoon sweet paprika

1 teaspoon ground cumin

12 fresh flat-leaf parsley sprigs, minced

Salt to taste

8 phyllo sheets

Vegetable oil for frying

Lemon wedges for garnish

Preheat the broiler. Place the peppers on a lightly oiled baking sheet and broil about 3 inches from the heat source, turning carefully with tongs, until the skins are evenly charred. Transfer them to a paper or plastic bag and close it. When the peppers are cool enough to handle, peel and seed them. Dice them coarsely and place in a colander to drain.

In a medium skillet over medium-high heat, heat the olive oil. Cook the onion, garlic, and paprika, stirring occasionally, until tender, 6 to 8 minutes. Transfer to a medium bowl. Add the cumin, diced peppers, and parsley. Season with salt. Set aside.

Place 8 sheets of phyllo on a flat surface covered with a damp cloth. Cut the phyllo in half vertically and horizontally. This will give you 32 rectangles of phyllo. Remove 2 rectangles. Cover the stacked phyllo with a damp towel. Using the double layer of phyllo, spoon 2 tablespoons of the pepper filling in the center of the rectangle. Fold over two opposing sides so that they slightly overlap in the center. Fold over the other two sides to make a 3-by-4-inch pastry. Place, seam-side down, on a baking sheet. Repeat until all the filling has been used.

Line another baking sheet with paper towels. Into a large skillet over medium-high heat, pour oil to a depth of a ½ inch. Heat it to 325°F, or until a piece of phyllo sizzles instantly when added. Fry the *boureks* on both sides until golden. Transfer them to the baking sheet to drain. Serve *immediately* with lemon wedges. Repeat to cook remaining *boureks.*

BREADS AND SANDWICHES

✦

NO MEAL IN THE MAGHREB WOULD BE COMPLETE WITHOUT BREAD. IN HIS BOOK, **AU SEUIL DE LA VIE MAROCAINE**, LOUIS BRUNOT QUOTES A MOROCCAN PROVERB, "Bread is a Godsend, and it is with bread that we live." A reverence for bread is much in evidence throughout North Africa to this day.

Whether in cities or in the countryside, most housewives still prepare their own bread before sending it to the neighborhood oven for baking. While the dense, round loaves called *kesra, khobz* ("hobz"), or *tabouna* still predominate in the Maghreb, the slender French baguette, a legacy of the most recent colonial period, is becoming increasingly popular. This has led some prominent food professionals to express concern for the survival of the wholesome traditional breads once found on every North African table.

MOUNA

SEPHARDIC EGG BREAD (ALGERIA)

MAKES 1 LARGE OR 2 MEDIUM LOAVES

MOUNA IS THE TRADITIONAL EGG BREAD EATEN DURING THE JEWISH SABBATH. IT IS DELICATELY SWEET AND HAS A TEXTURE SIMILAR TO FRENCH BRIOCHE. I LOVE TO DUNK A TOASTED SLICE OF FRESH **MOUNA** IN A STEAMING CUP OF CAFÉ AU LAIT! IN A VARIATION OF THIS RECIPE, SOME COOKS ENCLOSE SEVERAL HEAPING SPOONFULS OF SWEET PRESERVES IN THE CENTER OF THE DOUGH BEFORE BAKING. ALLOW SEVERAL HOURS FOR THE DOUGH TO RISE.

In a medium bowl, dissolve the yeast in the warm water. Stir in 2 teaspoons of the sugar and 1 cup of the flour. Mix well, cover, and set aside in a warm place until doubled, 45 minutes to 1 hour.

Meanwhile, in a large bowl, whisk (by hand or with a mixer equipped with a dough hook) ¾ cup of the sugar and 3 of the eggs until fairly smooth. Add the butter and mix well. Blend in the orange zest. Gradually add the remaining 3 cups flour and blend until smooth. Set aside.

When the yeast mixture has risen, add it to the egg and flour mixture and knead on a floured board until the dough is smooth and elastic to the touch, 8 to 10 minutes. Coat your hands with vegetable oil. Shape the kneaded dough into a large ball. Return it to the bowl and cover with a clean towel. Set it in a warm place until doubled, about 1 hour.

Lightly oil 2 baking sheets and sprinkle them with flour. Separate the dough into 2 equal parts and reshape them into balls. Place them on the baking sheets, cover, and let rise until doubled, about 1 hour.

Preheat the oven to 400°F. Beat the remaining egg with the cold water. Paint each dough ball with the egg wash. With a sharp knife, make 5 to 6 slits on the top of each loaf like spokes on a wheel. Sprinkle the loaves with the remaining sugar. Bake until golden brown, 12 to 15 minutes.

1 package active dry yeast

3 tablespoons warm (105° to 115°F) water

1 cup sugar

4 cups unbleached all-purpose flour

4 eggs

½ cup (1 stick) unsalted butter at room temperature, cut into pieces

Vegetable oil as needed

Grated zest of 1 orange

1 tablespoon cold water

FRICASSÉES

FRIED SANDWICHES (TUNISIA)

MAKES 14 TO 16 **FRICASSÉES**; SERVES 8 AS A MAIN COURSE

SINCE ANTIQUITY, TUNISIA HAS BEEN ONE OF THE WORLD LEADERS IN THE PRODUCTION OF OLIVE OIL. IN THE CITY OF SFAX, ON TUNISIA'S CENTRAL COAST, THE AIR IS HEAVY WITH THE PUNGENT SMELL OF OLIVE OIL THAT EMANATES FROM THE MORE THAN FOUR HUNDRED PROCESSING MILLS SCATTERED THROUGHOUT THE CITY. IN THE CENTER OF TOWN, YOUNG BOYS HAWK SMALL BOUQUETS OF JASMINE, WHILE VENDORS LINING THE ELEGANT ARCADES LEADING UP TO THE FORTIFIED MEDINA (OLD TOWN), TEMPT PASSERSBY WITH FRESHLY MADE **FRICASSÉES** DISPLAYED ON A BED OF PARSLEY. THE SMALL OVAL-SHAPED FRIED BREADS ARE A POPULAR STREET SNACK, AND ARE FILLED WITH A VARIETY OF INGREDIENTS SUCH AS COOKED GREEN PEPPERS AND CUBES OF POTATOES, CAPERS, AND HARD-COOKED EGGS. **FRICASSÉES** SHOULD BE SERVED WHILE THEY ARE STILL WARM, FOR THEY HAVE A TENDENCY TO TOUGHEN AS THEY COOL.

1 package active dry yeast

¼ cup plus 1 to 1½ cups warm (105° to 115°F) water

4 cups unbleached all-purpose flour

1 teaspoon salt, plus salt to taste

3 tablespoons olive oil, plus olive oil for frying

3 eggs

1 onion, thinly sliced

2 bell peppers, seeded, deribbed, and thinly sliced

1 boiling potato, peeled and cut into ½-inch cubes

2 teaspoons capers, drained

12 green olives, pitted and coarsely chopped

Salt and freshly ground black pepper to taste

Harissa (page 19), (optional)

In a small bowl, dilute the yeast in the ¼ cup warm water. Set aside until the mixture starts to bubble, 10 to 15 minutes.

In the bowl of a heavy-duty mixer with the dough hook in place, mix the flour and 1 teaspoon salt. Make a well in the center and pour in the yeast mixture, 1 tablespoon olive oil, and 1 lightly beaten egg. Knead, gradually adding the 1 to 1½ cups of warm water as needed. Continue kneading until the dough is smooth and elastic to the touch, about 8 to 10 minutes. To knead by hand, mix the flour with the salt in a large bowl. Make a well in the center and pour in the yeast mixture, 1 tablespoon olive oil, and one lightly beaten egg. Mix with a wooden spoon, gradually adding the water, until the dough leaves the sides of the bowl. Transfer the dough to a lightly floured work surface and knead until it becomes smooth and elastic to the touch, 8 to 10 minutes.

Coat your hands lightly with oil and shape the dough into a ball. Return it to the bowl. Cover it with a clean towel and let it rise in a warm place until doubled, about 1 hour. Punch the dough down, cover, and let rise again until doubled, about 1 hour.

Meanwhile, in a medium saucepan, boil the 2 remaining eggs for 12 to 15 minutes. Cool, then shell and mash the eggs coarsely. Set aside. In a medium skillet over medium heat, heat 2 tablespoons olive oil and cook the onion, peppers, and potato, stirring occasionally, until tender, 15 to 20 minutes. Transfer to a bowl and mix with the capers, olives, salt and pepper to taste, and hard-cooked eggs. Set aside.

Again rub oil on your hands to prevent the dough from sticking. Take ¼ cup of the dough and form it into an egg shape, flattening it slightly. Set aside on a platter. Continue in this manner until all the dough is used up. Into a deep-fat fryer or heavy pot, pour the olive oil to a depth of 3 inches. Heat it over medium-high heat until the oil is fragrant, or until a small piece of dough sizzles instantly when added. Line a baking sheet with paper towels. Drop the pieces of dough into the hot oil, in batches if necessary, and fry them until they are puffy and golden, about 5 to 6 minutes. Drain well on paper towels. While the *fricassées* are warm, slice them open and fill with the potato stuffing. Top with harissa, if using. Serve immediately.

SANDWICH TUNISIEN

BEN YEDDER SUBMARINE (TUNISIA)

MAKES 1 SANDWICH

PATISSERIE BEN YEDDER IS A POPULAR BAKERY AND CAFETERIA JUST A SHORT WALK FROM THE MARCHÉ CENTRAL IN DOWNTOWN TUNIS. THROUGHOUT THE DAY, A STEADY STREAM OF CUSTOMERS DROPS BY TO PURCHASE ONE OF THE **PATISSERIE'S** SPECIALTIES, A CRUSTY **PETIT PAIN** (FRENCH ROLL) BULGING WITH AN ASSORTMENT OF COOKED SALADS, RAW VEGETABLES, EGGS, GRILLED MEAT, TUNA FISH, AND CONDIMENTS THAT ARE ON DISPLAY BEHIND THE LONG GLASS DELI CASE. THE **PETIT PAIN** USED FOR THEIR RENOWNED **SANDWICH TUNISIEN** IS BAKED ON THE PREMISES. "THE AROMA OF THE BREAD ALONE PULLS MANY CUSTOMERS INTO OUR CAFETERIA," SAYS THE AMERICAN-EDUCATED SELIM BEN YEDDER, WHO DESCENDS FROM A LONG LINE OF TUNISIAN BAKERS. BE SURE TO DRIZZLE OLIVE OIL AND A LITTLE HARISSA OVER YOUR SANDWICH, THE WAY TUNISIANS DO.

One fresh, crusty 6-inch French roll

1 boiled potato, sliced

1 tomato, sliced

2 tablespoons mechwya (page 63)

2 tablespoons Ommok Houria
     (page 56)

2 tablespoons Cucumber and Tomato
     Salad (page 62)

6 green or black olives, pitted

2 teaspoons capers, drained (optional)

1 hard-cooked egg, sliced

Olive oil for drizzling

Harissa to taste (page 19)

Slice the roll in half lengthwise. Remove some of the soft dough from inside each half of the roll. On the bottom half, layer the potato and the tomato slices. Place 1 heaping tablespoon of each salad on top of the tomatoes. Top with olives, optional capers, and egg slices. Drizzle with olive oil. Dilute some harissa with water and sprinkle over the top. Replace the top half of the roll and serve.

MEDFOUNA

BERBER PIZZA (MOROCCO)

MAKES ONE 12-INCH **MEDFOUNA**

RISSANI IS A HISTORIC MOROCCAN TOWN ON THE EDGE OF THE SAHARA. FOR CENTURIES IT WAS THE ULTIMATE DESTINATION FOR CAMEL CARAVANS ARRIVING FROM THE SOUTH. IT IS ALSO WHERE MY HUSBAND AND I HAD OUR FIRST TASTE OF **MEDFOUNA**, A LOCAL SPECIALTY. ONCE, WHILE WANDERING THROUGH THE MEDINA (OLD TOWN), WE CAME UPON THE ENTRANCE TO THE TOWN'S PUBLIC OVEN. WE STEPPED DOWN THROUGH A NARROW OPENING INTO A CAVELIKE ROOM, LIT ONLY BY THE LIGHT FILTERING THROUGH THE DOORWAY AND THE EERIE GLOW FROM THE OVEN'S CHARCOAL FIRE. A YOUNG BOY SAT CROSS-LEGGED ON THE GROUND, DILIGENTLY CHOPPING THE INGREDIENTS FOR THE **MEDFOUNA** FILLING ON A LARGE BOARD. WITH A PRACTICED MOTION, HE SPREAD A LAYER OF MIXED HERBS AND VEGETABLES OVER ONE THICK CIRCLE OF DOUGH, QUICKLY COVERING THEM WITH ANOTHER. (**MEDFOUNA**, A SORT OF STUFFED PIZZA, MEANS "HIDDEN" IN ARABIC.) THE BAKER, USING A LONG-HANDLED WOODEN PADDLE, GENTLY LIFTED THE **MEDFOUNA** OFF THE BOARD AND SLID IT INTO THE OVEN. AFTER SOME HAGGLING OVER PRICE, AND A HALF-HOUR WAIT, WE MADE OFF WITH A WARM, GOLDEN, AND PERFECTLY DELICIOUS **MEDFOUNA**.

To make the dough: In a small bowl, dissolve the yeast in ¼ cup warm water. Add the sugar and let stand in a warm place until the mixture starts to bubble, about 10 or 15 minutes.

In the bowl of a heavy-duty mixer with the dough hook in place, mix the flour and salt. Make a well in the center and pour in the yeast mixture, the oil, and the egg. Knead, adding the oil and gradually adding the 1 to 1 ½ cups water as needed, until the dough is smooth and elastic to the touch, about 8 to 10 minutes. To knead by hand, mix the flour with the salt in a large bowl. Make a well in the center and pour in the yeast mixture, oil, and the egg. Mix with a wooden spoon or spatula, gradually adding the 1 to 1½ cups water, until the dough leaves the sides of the bowl. Transfer the dough to a lightly floured work surface and knead until it becomes smooth and elastic to the touch, 8 to 10 minutes. Grease 2 baking sheets and dust them with flour. Separate the dough into 2 balls of equal size and place each one on a baking sheet. Cover with a clean cloth and set aside in a warm place until doubled, about 1 hour.

Dough

1 package active dry yeast

¼ cup plus 1 to 1½ cups warm
(105° to 115°F) water

1 teaspoon sugar

4 cups unbleached all-purpose flour

1 teaspoon salt

2 tablespoons olive oil

1 egg, lightly beaten

Filling

2 tablespoons olive oil

8 green onions with tops, finely chopped

2 garlic cloves, minced

1 bell pepper, seeded, deribbed, and
    finely diced

12 green olives, pitted and minced

1 teaspoon sweet paprika

½ teaspoon ground cumin

½ teaspoon ground turmeric

½ teaspoon dried thyme

Salt and freshly ground black pepper
    to taste

Olive oil for brushing

Meanwhile, to make the filling: In a large skillet over medium heat, heat the olive oil. Cook the green onions, garlic, and bell pepper, stirring occasionally, until tender, 6 to 8 minutes. Add the olives, paprika, cumin, turmeric, thyme, salt, and pepper. Set aside.

Preheat the oven to 425°F. Lightly grease a 12-inch pizza pan and sprinkle it with a little flour. On a work surface dusted with flour, roll one ball of dough into a circle 12 inches in diameter. Carefully lift the circle onto the pizza pan and spread it evenly with the filling. Roll the second ball into a 12-inch circle and place it on top of the filling. Seal the edges. Brush the top with olive oil. Bake for 10 minutes. Lower the heat to 375°F and bake until the crust is golden, 20 to 25 minutes. Let cool slightly on a wire rack. When the *medfouna* is cool enough to handle, cut it into wedges and serve.

KESRA

MOROCCAN BREAD

MAKES 2 LOAVES

BY THE TIME THEY REACH SCHOOL AGE, YOUNG GIRLS THROUGHOUT NORTH AFRICA ARE ADEPT IN THE ART OF BREAD MAKING. FOR ECONOMIC AND, SOME MIGHT SAY, SPIRITUAL REASONS, MANY FAMILIES STILL MAKE THEIR OWN BREAD ON A DAILY BASIS, EVEN THOUGH TRADITIONAL BREADS, AS WELL AS FRENCH BAGUETTES AND **PETITS PAINS**, ARE AVAILABLE AT MOST BAKERIES. WHENEVER I VISIT OUR HOME WITHIN THE RAMPARTS OF THE ANCIENT MEDINA OF AZEMMOUR, I DELIGHT IN WATCHING THE DAILY PROCESSION OF YOUNG CHILDREN TAKING THEIR FAMILY'S UNBAKED LOAVES TO THE COMMUNITY OVEN. AROUND LUNCHTIME, AND AGAIN IN THE EARLY EVENING, THE TANTALIZING AROMA OF FRESHLY BAKED BREAD WAFTS THROUGH THE LABYRINTHINE STREETS, SENDING AN OLFACTORY SIGNAL THAT THE **KESRA** IS READY. SOON, CHATTERING GROUPS OF YOUNG CHILDREN GATHER AT THE DOOR OF THE BAKERY TO RETRIEVE THEIR PLUMP LOAVES FROM ROUGH WOODEN SHELVES, EACH LOAF BEARING THE FAMILY'S DISTINGUISHING MARK. IN TRADITIONAL MOROCCAN HOUSEHOLDS, CHUNKS OF WARM BREAD ARE USED IN PLACE OF SILVERWARE TO SCOOP UP MORSELS OF FOOD FROM THE COMMUNAL DISH. FOR SPECIAL CELEBRATIONS, **KESRA** IS FLAVORED WITH WHOLE ANISEEDS OR SESAME SEEDS. YOU CAN USE WHOLE-WHEAT FLOUR OR A BLEND OF WHOLE-WHEAT AND WHITE FLOURS, IF YOU PREFER.

In a small bowl, mix the yeast with the ¼ cup warm water. Stir in the sugar. Set aside until the mixture starts to bubble, 10 to 15 minutes.

In the bowl of a heavy-duty mixer with the dough hook in place, mix the flour, ⅓ cup of the cornmeal, and salt. Make a well in the center and pour in the yeast mixture and melted butter. Knead, gradually adding the remaining 2 cups water as needed, until the dough is smooth and elastic to the touch, for 8 or 10 minutes. To knead by hand, mix the flour with the ⅓ cup cornmeal and salt in a large bowl. Make a well in the center, and pour in the yeast mixture and melted butter. Mix with a wooden spoon, gradually adding the 1 to 1¼ cups water as needed, until the dough leaves the sides of the bowl. Transfer the dough to a lightly floured work surface and knead until it becomes smooth and elastic to the touch, 8 to 10 minutes. Grease 2 baking sheets and dust them with the 1 tablespoon cornmeal. Separate the dough into 2 balls of equal size and set each ball on a baking sheet. Press them into circles 8 inches in diameter. Sprinkle 1

1 package active dry yeast

¼ cup plus 2 cups warm
   (105° to 115°F) water

1 teaspoon sugar

4 cups unbleached all-purpose flour

⅓ cup cornmeal plus 1 tablespoon
   for dusting

2 teaspoons salt

2 tablespoons unsalted butter, melted

2 teaspoons sesame seeds

teaspoon of the sesame seeds over each loaf, gently pressing them into the dough. Cover the dough with a clean towel and set aside in a warm place until doubled, about 1 hour.

Preheat the oven to 425°F. Prick the top of each *kesra* with the tines of a fork. Bake for 10 minutes. Lower the heat to 375°F and bake until crusty and golden, 15 to 20 minutes.

chapter eight

DESSERTS AND
BEVERAGES

DESSERTS AND BEVERAGES

DESSERTS

THANKS TO A MILD MEDITERRANEAN CLIMATE, THE INHABITANTS OF THE MAGHREB ENJOY A WIDE VARIETY OF FRUITS THE YEAR AROUND. THIS EXPLAINS WHY THE MOST POPULAR DESSERT IS ALSO THE SIMPLEST: A PLATTER OF SEASONAL FRESH FRUIT.

In the spring and summer, the variety of regionally grown fruit found in North African souks and markets is much like that found in American supermarkets: strawberries, bananas, cherries, peaches, plums, apricots, and figs, as well as several varieties of melons. Fall is the season for crisp apples and pears brought in from the mountain regions, and for ruby-red pomegranates and tart quinces. This is also the time to sample the year's crop of dates grown in the region's desert oases. Winter brings an abundance of citrus, such as blood oranges bursting with crimson juice, as well as small, sweet tangerines, which were named for the people of Tangier in northern Morocco.

At the end of an elaborate meal marking a special occasion, a second dessert course may follow the fruit tray. Sometimes it is *mhalbi,* a custardlike dish fragrant with rose or orange flower water. An array of honey-coated pastries or plump dates stuffed with almond paste might also be served.

LOQMA

FRIED HONEY PUFFS (ALGERIA)

MAKES ABOUT 18 **LOQMA**; SERVES 4 TO 6

WHEN FRIED TO A GOLDEN BROWN AND DIPPED IN HONEY, THESE LIGHT DOUGHNUTS ARE SIMILAR TO GREEK **LOUKOUMATHES** AND TAKE ON THE APPEARANCE OF GLAZED APRICOTS. ALSO FOUND IN TUNISIA, WHERE THEY ARE SOMETIMES CALLED **BOULES AU MIEL**, THEY ARE OFTEN SERVED AS AN AFTERNOON SNACK ALONG WITH A GLASS OF MINT TEA OR A CUP OF CAFÉ AU LAIT. THEY SHOULD BE FRIED AS CLOSE TO SERVING TIME AS POSSIBLE.

In a medium saucepan, combine the water, butter, sugar, and salt. Bring to a boil and stir until the butter melts. Remove from the heat. With a wooden spoon, stir in the flour all at once and continue stirring until the mixture is smooth. Add the eggs, one at a time, incorporating each one until the dough is completely smooth. Let the dough rest for 15 minutes.

Meanwhile, in a medium saucepan, bring the honey to a boil. Add the orange zest, orange juice, and orange flower water. Lower the heat and keep the mixture simmering on the stove.

Into a heavy pot or a deep-fat fryer, pour oil to a depth of 2 inches. Heat it over medium-high heat to 350°F, or until a piece of dough dropped into the oil sizzles instantly. Drop the dough by tablespoonfuls into the hot oil. Fry in batches until the dough balls puff up and turn golden brown, about 3 or 4 minutes. With a slotted spoon, transfer them to paper towels to drain. While they are still hot, using tongs or a slotted spoon, gently lower them into the saucepan of simmering honey. Coat them with the hot honey. Transfer to a serving dish and serve as soon as all the *loqma* are fried.

1 cup water

2 tablespoons unsalted butter

2 tablespoons sugar

½ teaspoon salt

1 cup unbleached all-purpose flour

4 eggs

1 cup honey

Grated zest of 1 orange

¼ cup orange juice

1 teaspoon orange flower water

Vegetable oil for frying

TMAR M'HAMMAR BI LOOZ MET'HOON

DATES STUFFED WITH ALMOND PASTE (MOROCCO, ALGERIA, TUNISIA)

MAKES ABOUT 20 TO 24 STUFFED DATES

DATES, A STAPLE OF THE NORTH AFRICAN DIET, ALSO HAVE SYMBOLIC MEANING FOR THE PEOPLE OF THE MAGHREB. IT IS THEIR CUSTOM TO WELCOME A GUEST TO THEIR HOME WITH A SMALL PLATE OF DATES AND A GLASS OF MILK. DURING THE MOSLEM OBSERVANCE OF RAMADAN, DATES ACCOMPANY THE FIRST BOWL OF SOUP SERVED EACH EVENING TO BREAK THE DAY'S FAST. FOR DESSERT, PLUMP RIPE DATES ARE OFTEN STUFFED WITH ALMOND PASTE TINTED WITH GREEN FOOD COLORING. THE BEST DATES FOR STUFFING ARE THE LARGE MEDJOOLS, NATIVE TO ALGERIA AND MOROCCO. FORTUNATELY, THEY ARE ALSO GROWN IN CALIFORNIA'S COACHELLA VALLEY, NEAR PALM SPRINGS (SEE PAGE 156 FOR A SOURCE OF FRESH MEDJOOLS).

7 ounces almond paste

1 tablespoon orange flower water

2 or 3 drops green food coloring
  (optional)

24 Medjool dates, sliced open
  (not cut in half) and pitted

1 cup powdered sugar, sifted

½ cup colored sugar crystals (optional)

Grated zest of 1 orange

In a medium bowl, using your fingers, mix the almond paste with the orange flower water and the food coloring, if using. Take 1 heaping teaspoon of almond paste and form it into a spindle shape. Stuff the date with the almond paste spindle (it should bulge out slightly from the date). Roll the stuffed date in a saucer filled with the optional colored sugar crystals. Set the date in a fluted paper cup or on a platter and garnish with orange zest. Repeat with the remaining dates.

PHYLLO PURSES WITH CUSTARD SAUCE

MAKES 10 PURSES

THIS IS MY ADAPTATION OF THE SWEET **BRIOUAT** PASTRIES SOMETIMES SERVED AT THE END OF A NORTH AFRICAN BANQUET.

Preheat the oven to 400°F. Grate the zest of the orange and squeeze the juice. Set aside. In a medium saucepan, combine the raisins, figs, and water. Bring to a simmer and cook, covered, until the fruit is plump, 8 to 10 minutes. Add the dates, cinnamon, nuts, and freshly squeezed orange juice. Mix until the liquid is absorbed. Remove from the heat and stir in the orange flower water. Set aside.

In a double boiler over simmering water, whisk the egg yolks with the sugar and the cornstarch until they turn pale yellow. Gradually whisk in the milk and cook, stirring continuously with a wooden spoon, until the custard coats the back of the spoon, 15 to 20 minutes. Stir in the almond extract and remove from the heat. Set aside.

Set the 6 sheets of phyllo on a damp cloth. Cut them in half lengthwise. Place the halved sheets on top of each other and cut in half crosswise. This will give you 24 small sheets of phyllo. Separate 2 sheets from the stack. Cover the stack with a damp cloth. With a pastry brush, brush 1 sheet with butter and set it on a flat surface. Brush the second sheet of phyllo and lay it on top of the first to form a cross. In the center of this cross, place ¼ cup of the fruit filling. Enclose the filling with the phyllo, lightly twisting the top to form a small purse. Place on a lightly greased or nonstick baking sheet. Proceed in a similar manner until all the filling is used. Bake the pastries until lightly golden, 10 to 12 minutes.

To serve, place 1 pastry in the center of each dessert plate. Spoon some of the custard over and around each one. Garnish with orange zest. Serve warm or at room temperature.

1 large Valencia orange

2 cups (12 ounces) golden raisins

10 dried Mission figs

½ cup water

1 cup (6 ounces) pitted dates, chopped

¼ teaspoon ground cinnamon

½ cup almonds, pistachios, or walnuts, crushed

1 tablespoon orange flower water

4 large egg yolks

2 tablespoons sugar

1 tablespoon cornstarch

1½ cups milk

¼ teaspoon almond extract

6 sheets phyllo dough

1 cup (2 sticks) unsalted butter, melted

Grated orange zest for garnish

MHALBI

CUSTARD WITH ORANGE FLOWER WATER (MOROCCO, ALGERIA, TUNISIA)

SERVES 5

MHALBI IN TUNISIA, OR **MULHALBIA** IN MOROCCO, IS A SWEET, CUSTARDLIKE DESSERT POPULAR THROUGHOUT NORTH AFRICA AND THE MIDDLE EAST. MOROCCANS AND ALGERIANS USE ORANGE FLOWER WATER OR ROSE WATER TO FLAVOR THIS DESSERT, WHILE TUNISIANS ADD A FRAGRANT LIQUID DISTILLED FROM ROSE GERANIUMS. IN MOROCCO, THE CUSTARD IS OFTEN SERVED IN A COMMUNAL DISH SET IN THE CENTER OF THE TABLE AND GARNISHED WITH GROUND ALMONDS AND CINNAMON. IN TUNISIA, IT IS USUALLY SERVED IN INDIVIDUAL PARFAIT GLASSES AND TOPPED WITH PINE NUTS OR CRUSHED PISTACHIOS.

⅓ cup cornstarch

3 cups milk

¼ cup sugar

1 cinnamon stick

2 tablespoons orange flower, rose, or rose
    geranium water

½ cup almonds, toasted pine nuts
    (page 24), or pistachio nuts, ground

2 cups fresh raspberries (optional)

In a small bowl, dilute the cornstarch with ½ cup of the milk. Set aside. In a heavy, medium saucepan, bring the remaining 2½ cups milk, sugar, and cinnamon stick to a boil. Add the cornstarch mixture. Whisk continuously until the mixture thickens, about 5 minutes. Remove from the heat and remove the cinnamon stick. Stir in the orange flower, rose, or rose geranium water. Pour into 5 individual ramekins or parfait glasses. Let cool.

    Sprinkle with the nuts and garnish with fresh raspberries, if using. Serve chilled or at room temperature.

TMAR KWEERAT

FATIMA'S DATE AND ALMOND TRUFFLES (MOROCCO)

MAKES ABOUT TWENTY 1-INCH TRUFFLES

SEVERAL YEARS AGO, I WAS ASKED TO SERVE ON A PANEL OF JUDGES AT A MOROCCAN NATIONAL CULINARY COMPETITION IN THE BEAUTIFUL CITY OF AGADIR, A POPULAR BEACH RESORT IN SOUTHERN MOROCCO. MY FELLOW JUDGES AND I SAMPLED NUMEROUS VARIATIONS OF COUSCOUS AND **TAGINE** FOR THE BETTER PART OF THREE DAYS. WE UNANIMOUSLY SELECTED AS OUR FIRST-PRIZE WINNER FATIMA IDDOUCHE, A YOUNG WOMAN FROM SAFI, WHO WAS THE HEAD CHEF AT A LOCAL HOTEL. HER WINNING RECIPE WAS A **TAGINE** OF LAMB IN HONEY SAUCE THAT SHE HAD GARNISHED WITH THESE AMBROSIAL DATE AND ALMOND TRUFFLES. THE TRUFFLES ARE ALSO DELICIOUS SERVED ON THEIR OWN FOR DESSERT.

1½ cups (7 ounces) slivered almonds, toasted (see page 24)
1 cup (6 ounces) pitted dates, chopped
1 tablespoon orange flower water
1 tablespoon honey
½ teaspoon ground cinnamon
½ cup shredded coconut

Place half of the toasted almonds and the dates in a blender or food processor and grind them coarsely to a thick paste; repeat to grind the remaining almonds and dates. Transfer it to a medium bowl. With your hands, blend in the orange flower water, honey, and cinnamon. Shape into 1-inch balls.

On a plate sprinkled with coconut, roll the balls until they are evenly coated. Place them in miniature fluted paper cups. They will keep for up to 1 month in an airtight container in the refrigerator. Serve chilled or at room temperature.

ROMMAN BI NAHNA

POMEGRANATE AND MINT CUP (MOROCCO)

SERVES 4

IN SEASON, THE BRIGHT RED FRUIT OF THE POMEGRANATE, A SYMBOL OF FERTILITY IN GREEK AND ROMAN TIMES, DECORATES THE GARDENS OF MANY NORTH AFRICAN HOMES. IN TUNISIA, THE RUBY-COLORED SEEDS ARE MIXED WITH COUSCOUS FOR DESSERT. IN MOROCCO, A TALL GLASS OF FRESH POMEGRANATE JUICE FLAVORED WITH A DASH OF ORANGE FLOWER WATER IS A REFRESHING BEVERAGE MUCH APPRECIATED ON A WARM DAY. BUT I LOVE THE BLEND OF FLAVORS AND TEXTURES IN THIS RECIPE GIVEN TO ME BY BOUCHAIB MARZOUK, WHO LIVES IN AZEMMOUR. SELECT THE RIPEST AND SWEETEST POMEGRANATES POSSIBLE FOR THIS LUSCIOUS DESSERT.

In a serving bowl, mix the pomegranate seeds with the yogurt and the mint. Garnish with mint sprigs.

NOTE: To minimize stains when peeling a pomegranate, fill a sink or a large bowl with water. Hold the fruit under water, cut open the crown, score the skin lightly into quarters, and peel it away carefully. The seeds will sink to the bottom while the pith floats to the top. Pour off the water, drain the fruit, and proceed with the recipe.

3 ripe pomegranates
1 cup (8 ounces) vanilla yogurt
10 fresh mint leaves, finely minced
Fresh mint sprigs for garnish

CHALADA FAWAKEEH BI MA Z'HAR

ORANGE FLOWER FRUIT CUP (MOROCCO, ALGERIA, TUNISIA)

SERVES 4

ONE OF THE MOST POPULAR DESSERTS IN NORTH AFRICA, AND ONE OF MY FAVORITES, IS THIS LIGHT, REFRESHING, AND FRAGRANT FRUIT SALAD LIBERALLY SPRINKLED WITH ORANGE FLOWER WATER. IN TUNISIA, ROSE GERANIUM WATER IS SUBSTITUTED FOR THE ORANGE FLOWER WATER.

2 tart apples, peeled, cored, and finely diced

2 crisp pears, peeled, cored, and finely diced

1 orange, peeled, seeded, sectioned, and finely chopped

2 bananas, finely diced

2 peaches, plums, or nectarines, peeled and finely diced

1 tablespoon orange flower water

½ teaspoon ground cinnamon

Fresh mint sprigs for garnish

Mix the fruit and the orange flower water together in a serving bowl. Sprinkle with cinnamon. Chill. Garnish with mint sprigs to serve.

BEVERAGES

NORTH AFRICANS ENJOY A VARIETY OF BEVERAGES, FROM THE JUICE OF RIPE WATERMELON TO THAT OF SWEET POMEGRANATES OR FRESHLY PICKED ORANGES. THE MOST POPULAR DRINK IN THE REGION, HOWEVER, IS MINT TEA.

Throughout the Maghreb, everyone enjoys a steaming glass of mint tea, whether at a sidewalk cafe, in a modern office building, under a nomad's tent, or in the bazaars of Marrakech or Tunis. As anyone who has visited the region knows, a glass of mint tea is an inextricable part of any negotiating process. It is also offered as a sign of welcome.

Abderrahim Bargache, noted Moroccan television host and food historian, points out the social significance of mint tea in *La grande Encyclopédie du Maroc:* "From the poorest to the wealthiest, there isn't a single household where the visitor won't be offered at least one, if not several glasses of mint tea. Indeed, the worst insult one can bestow upon a miser or a boor is: 'May God protect us: in this man's home, we weren't even given a glass of tea!'"

Preparing and serving mint tea to guests involves a ritual usually performed by the man of the house. Seated cross-legged on the floor facing the tray bearing the necessary implements and ingredients, he first pours a little boiling water into a pot-bellied teapot to warm it. After discarding the water, he carefully measures the correct amount of green tea, placing it in the pot before filling it with boiling water. He allows the tea to steep for several minutes. Then he stuffs the pot with as much fresh mint as it will hold. Using a small silver hammer, he breaks off chunks from a conical sugar loaf. He adds a generous quantity of these to the tea to give it an almost syrupy consistency. To test aroma and flavor, he pours some into a glass and takes a sip. If it meets with his approval, he fills a number of decorative glasses, alternately lowering and elevating the teapot as he pours, sometimes from a height of several feet. The tea is ready to be served.

Alys Lowth in *A Wayfarer in Morocco,* recounts that guests too, are bound by tradition: Three glasses of tea should be consumed before they can take their leave. "The moment our glass of tea has been emptied, the host refills it, and at least three must be taken or no good fortune will follow."

ATAY BI NAHNA

MINT TEA (MOROCCO, ALGERIA, TUNISIA)

SERVES 4 TO 6

CHINESE GUNPOWDER GREEN TEA AND COMMON BACKYARD MINT, **MENTHA VERIDIS**, ARE USED TO MAKE MINT TEA IN MOROCCO. THE TEA IS SWEETENED WITH A GENEROUS AMOUNT OF SUGAR. A FRESH ORANGE BLOSSOM OR A TINY JASMINE FLOWER ADDED TO EACH GLASS WILL ENHANCE THE ALREADY FRAGRANT DRINK. IN TUNISIA, GREEN TEA IS BOILED ALONG WITH DRIED MINT TO YIELD A DEEP AMBER-COLORED BEVERAGE. AT THE CAFÉ DES NATTES IN SIDI BOU SAÏD OUTSIDE TUNIS, TOASTED PINE NUTS ARE FLOATED IN THE TEA TO PROVIDE A FINAL TOUCH. IN SOME PARTS OF ALGERIA, ROASTED PEANUTS ARE TRADITIONALLY SERVED ON THE SIDE.

Place the tea in a teapot and fill it with the boiling water. Let the tea steep for 2 minutes. Rinse the mint under running water and pack it into the teapot. Stir in the sugar. Serve hot.

2 teaspoons Chinese Gunpowder tea

5 cups boiling water

15 fresh mint sprigs

Sugar to taste

BOISSON AUX FRAISES

KELIBIA SMOOTHIE (TUNISIA)

SERVES I

STOP! CAFÉ MAURE! SAID A SIGN THAT CAUGHT MY ATTENTION ON THE STEEP ROAD TO THE IMPOS-
ING SIXTH-CENTURY FORTRESS OF KELIBIA, AT THE TIP OF TUNISIA'S CAP BON PENINSULA. I
OBEYED THE SIGN, AND STEPPED INTO THE MODEST OPEN-AIR CAFÉ OVERLOOKING THE SEA, WHERE I
TOOK A SEAT ON A STRAW MAT IN FRONT OF A LOW, ROUND TABLE. THE HOUSE SPECIALTY WAS THIS
WONDERFULLY REFRESHING STRAWBERRY DRINK. OVER THE NEXT HOUR, I HAD SEVERAL GLASSES WHILE
BREATHING IN THE PINE-SCENTED AIR AND ENJOYING THE MAGNIFICENT VIEW OF THE SCINTILLATING
BLUE WATERS OF THE MEDITERRANEAN.

2 tablespoons fresh lemon juice

1 cup water

½ cup fresh or frozen strawberries

2 teaspoons orange flower water

Sugar to taste

1 fresh mint sprigs for garnish

In a blender, mix the lemon juice, water, strawberries, orange flower water, and
sugar. Pour over ice into a tall glass. Decorate with a sprig of mint.

MAIL-ORDER SOURCES

OASIS BRANDS

P.O. Box 12871

La Jolla, CA 92039

619 276-1440

A Tunisian-owned company specializing in *tabil*, harissa blends, and other specialty foods.

OASIS DATE GARDENS

59–111 Highway 111

P.O. Box 757

Thermal, CA 92274

800 827-8017

California-grown Medjool dates and many other unusual varieties. Catalogue.

THE SPICE HOUSE

103 N. Old World Third Street

Milwaukee, WI 53203

414 272-0977

Spices from around the world, including Tunisian *tabil*. Catalogue.

KALUSTYAN ORIENT EXPORT CO.

123 Lexington Avenue

New York, NY 10016

212 685-3451

Spices.

VANNS SPICES LTD.

1238 Joppa Road

Baltimore, MD 21286

410 583-1643

Spices and spice blends.

GREATER GALILEE GOURMET, INC.

2118 Wilshire Boulevard, Suite 829

Santa Monica, CA 90403

800 290-1391

Olives imported from North Africa and the Middle East, olive oils, and spice blends. Newsletter.

BELLA CUCINA

5579 Peachtree Road

Atlanta, GA 30341

404 452-1819

Preserved lemons and olive oils.

CORNWALL BRIDGE POTTERY

Route 128

West Cornwall, CT 06796

203 672-6545

Lead-free Moroccan *tagine* dishes made to order.

VOLUBILIS IMPORTS

P.O. Box 2393

San Diego, CA 92038

619 530-0303

An importer of Moroccan wines. Call or write for list of sales locations.

NOMADS OF SANTA FE

207 Shelby Street

Santa Fe, NM 87501

505 986-0855

Moroccan imports, including *tagine* dishes.

MENUS

A FAMILY-STYLE LUNCH
Assiette Tunisienne (Tunisian Salad Plate)
Makhouda aux Epinards (Crustless Spinach Quiche)
Foul Mudammas (Fava Bean Stew with Olives)
Kesra (Moroccan Bread)
Fresh seasonal fruit and dates
Atay bi Nahna (Mint Tea)

AN ELEGANT MEAL
Cashew Bastila (Cashew Phyllo Pie)
Couscous aux Fenouils Meherzia
(Meherzia's Couscous with Fennel)
Mhalbi (Custard with Orange Flower Water)
Fresh seasonal fruit and dates
Atay bi Nahna (Mint Tea)

A DINNER FOR ENTERTAINING
An assortment of seasonal salads
Tagine Batata, Jilbana wa Kelbkok
(Tagine of Potatoes, Peas, and Artichoke Hearts)
Couscous Kabyle (Couscous from the Kabylie Region)
Tmar M'hammar bi Looz Met'hoon
(Dates Stuffed with Almond Paste)
Fresh seasonal fruit
Atay bi Nahna (Mint Tea)

A PICNIC
Medfouna (Berber Pizza)
Grilled Vegetable Kabobs with Charmoula Marinade
Tmar Kweerat (Fatima's Date and Almond Truffles)
Fruit juice

A LIGHT SUPPER
Harira (Lentil and Garbanzo Bean Soup)
Egg Breiks (Tunisian Egg Turnovers)
Chalada Fawakeeh bi Ma Z'har
(Orange Flower Fruit Cup)
Atay bi Nahna (Mint Tea)

A FAMILY SUPPER
Three-Bean Berkouksh (Bean and Pastini Soup)
Kefta aux Oeufs
(Vegetarian Meatballs with Eggs in Tomato Sauce)
Kesra (Moroccan Bread)
Romman bi Nahna (Pomegranate and Mint Cup)
Atay bi Nahna (Mint Tea)

A WINTER LUNCH OR DINNER
Ojja à la Courge (Tunisian Pumpkin Scramble)
Spaghetti Kerkennaise
(Spaghetti with Fresh Tomato and Caper Sauce)
Phyllo Purses with Custard Sauce
Fresh seasonal fruit
Atay bi Nahna (Mint Tea)

A SUMMER MEAL
Chef Ahmed's Eggs Malsouka (Egg and Spinach Pie)
Khalota (Vegetable Medley)
Fresh seasonal fruit
Atay bi Nahna (Mint Tea)

GLOSSARY

⊛

ATAY: Tea.

ATAY BI NAHNA: Mint tea.

BASTILA: Also spelled *b'stila* (phonetic Arabic), *pastilla* (French), or *besteeya* (English). A pastry consisting of layers of phyllolike dough enfolding a mixture of shredded fowl, fresh herbs, ground almonds, sugar, cinnamon, and eggs.

BERKOUKSH (OR BERKOK): Small pasta pellets marketed as acini di pepe in Italian markets. In French they are called *petits plombs,* or lead pellets.

BESSARA: Bean puree flavored with cumin and garlic.

BETZEL: See *briouat.*

BHARAT: A Tunisian blend of ground rosebuds, cinnamon, and black pepper.

BISMILLAH: "In the name of God!" Traditional invocation given at the beginning of a meal in a Moslem home.

BOUREK: Savory Algerian baked turnovers.

BREIK: Also spelled *brik.* A Tunisian fried turnover made from a thin, phyllolike dough, filled with an egg, tuna fish, or ground meat, and flavored with herbs and spices.

BRIOUAT: A Moroccan deep-fried or baked phyllo pastry. It can be cylindrical or triangular in shape, and may enclose either a savory or sweet filling.

CANOUN: A small charcoal brazier used in Morocco to cook *tagines.*

CHAKCHOUKA, CHOUCHOUKA, OR TCHACHOUKA: A fried green pepper and tomato mixture.

CHARMOULA (MOROCCO) OR M'CHARML (ALGERIA): A sauce made of olive oil, garlic, paprika, cumin, lemon juice (or vinegar), and cilantro, and used as a marinade for seafood. In Tunisia, *charmoula* (also *tchermila*) is made from caramelized onions, raisins, and a dash of vinegar.

CHORBA: Soup. Also the angel hair pasta used to thicken soups.

CHOUCH WARD: Dried rosebuds used in the Tunisian *bharat* spice blend.

CILANTRO: Fresh coriander or Chinese parsley (see *kesbor*).

CORIANDER SEEDS: The main ingredient in the Tunisian spice blend called *tabil.*

COUSCOUS: A staple of the North African diet made from cracked durum wheat, or semolina, that has been rolled into tiny pellets. Also the name for the finished dish.

COUSCOUSSIER (FRENCH): Sometimes spelled *couscoussiere.* A utensil that consists of a large soup pot topped with a tight-fitting colander. It is used to prepare couscous.

DIFFA: A Moroccan feast or banquet.

DIOUL: A phyllolike dough used to make Algerian appetizers and pastries.

DERSA: A blend of crushed red pepper, cumin, salt, and garlic that is used to flavor many Algerian dishes.

FOUL (PRONOUNCED "FULL"): Fava beans.

FOUL MUDAMMAS: Also spelled *m'dammes.* Small, brown-skinned fava beans.

GARBANZO BEANS: Also called chickpeas.

HARISSA: A Tunisian hot sauce usually made from dried red peppers, garlic, *tabil,* and olive oil.

HLELEM: Orzolike pasta pellets used to thicken soups in Tunisia.

HROUSS: A Tunisian hot sauce made from red peppers, onions, and spices.

KEFTA: Traditionally, a mixture of ground meat and herbs.

KEMIA: Appetizers.

KESBOUR OR KESBOR: Fresh coriander (cilantro). Used liberally in Algerian and Moroccan cuisine.

KESKES: Coucous pot.

KESRA: Leavened Moroccan bread.

KHALOTA (PRONOUNCED "HĂLŌTA"): An Algerian vegetable medley.

KHODRA (PRONOUNCED "HŌDRĂ"): Vegetables.

LOUBIA: Dried beans. Also the name of an Algerian bean soup.

MAGHREB: The name given to the northwestern African region that includes Morocco, Algeria, and Tunisia.

MAKHOUDA: A crustless quiche from Tunisia.

MALSOUKA: See *dioul.*

MANTECAOS: Algerian sweet or savory macaroonlike pastries.

MECHWYA: Tunisian grilled-pepper salad.

MEDINA: Old city.

MERGUEZ: A spicy Tunisian lamb sausage.

MOUNA: Jewish egg bread from Algeria.

NAHNA: Common backyard mint (*Mentha veridis*); used in mint tea.

OJJA: A Tunisian dish of scrambled eggs with peppers or other vegetables.

OUARKA: See *dioul* and *malsouka.*

PIEDS-NOIRS: North Africans of European descent.

RAMADAN: The annual Moslem month of fasting that commemorates the first revelation of the Koran.

SMEN: Aged butter used to flavor couscous and stews.

SOUK: An open-air market.

S'FFA: A very fine couscous, usually served as a dessert.

TABIL: Coriander seed.

TABIL, TAWABIL, OR TABIL KARWYA: A Tunisian spice blend of ground caraway, ground coriander seed, red pepper flakes, and dehydrated garlic.

TAGINE: Also spelled *tajine.* An exotic Moroccan and Algerian stew. Also in Morocco, the name of the earthenware utensil with a distinctive conical lid, in which the stew is prepared. In Tunisia, *tagine* refers to a crustless quiche similar to *makhouda.*

TBIKHA (PRONOUNCED "TBĒHĂ"): An Algerian vegetable medley.

BIBLIOGRAPHY

Ayache, Albert. *Histoire ancienne de l'Afrique du Nord.* Paris: Editions Sociales, 1964.

Bolens, Lucie. *La Cuisine andalouse: un art de vivre, XIe-XIIIe siècle.* Paris: Editions Albin Michel, 1990.

Bouayed, Fatima-Zohra. *La Cuisine algérienne.* Alger: ENAG Editions, 1991.

Brunot, Louis. *Au seuil de la vie marocaine.* Casablanca: Librairie Farairre, 1950.

Buffa, John, M.D., J.J. *Travels through the Empire of Morocco.* London: Stockdale, 1810.

Dagher, Shawky M., ed. *Traditional Foods in the Near East.* FAO Food and Nutrition Paper, no. 50. Rome: Food and Agriculture Organization of the United Nations, 1991.

Dinia, Hayat. *La Cuisine marocaine de Rabat.* Casablanca: Impression Idéale, 1990.

El Maleh, Edmond Amran. Quoted with permission, from a lecture on the art of Moroccan cuisine at the Premier Festival National des Arts Culinaires, Agadir, Morocco, February 1990.

Guinaudeau-Franc, Zette. *Les Secrets des cuisines en terre marocaine.* Paris: Jean-Pierre Taillandier Sochepress, 1981.

Hadjiat, Salima. *La Cuisine d'Algérie.* Paris: Collection Cuisine du Monde, Publisud, 1990.

Karsenty, Irène and Lucienne. *Le Livre de la cuisine Pied-Noir.* Paris: Editions Planète, 1969.

Kouki, Mohammed. *Cuisine et pâtisserie tunisiennes.* Tunis: Imprimerie Tunis-Carthage, 1993.

La grande Encyclopédie du Maroc, vol. 2. Rabat: 1988.

Lakhal, Naima. "La Production et la consommation de couscous au Maroc: de l'artisanat à l'industrie." Ph.D. dissertation, University of Toulouse-Le Mirail, 1988.

Loti, Pierre. *Into Morocco.* New York: Welch, Fracker & Company, 1889.

Lowth, Alys. *A Wayfarer in Morocco.* London: Methuen and Co., 1929.

Malapert, Lucienne. A la Recherche de l'Afrique romaine. Casablanca: Guide Marabout, 1975.

Moryoussef, Viviane and Nina. *La Cuisine juive marocaine.* Casablanca: Jean-Pierre Taillandier Sochepress, 1983.

Obeida, Khadidja. *253 Recettes de cuisine algérienne.* Paris: Jacques Grancher, Editeur, 1983.

Pellow, Thomas. *The Adventures of Thomas Pellow, Of Penryn, Mariner: Three and Twenty Years in Captivity Among the Moors, Written by Himself.* London: T. Fisher Unwin, 1890.

Rohlfs, Gerhard Dr. *Adventures in Morocco and Journeys through the Oases of Draa and Tafilet.* London: Sampson Low, Marston, Low and Searle, 1874.

Stone, Caroline. "Morocco Mouthfuls." *Aramco World 39,* November-December 1988.

Tamzali, Haydée. *La Cuisine en Afrique du Nord.* Hammamet, Tunisia: Michael Tomkinson Publishing, 1990.

Westermarck, Edward. *Ritual and Belief in Morocco.* London: MacMillan and Co., 1926.

Zeitoun, Edmond. *250 Recettes classiques de cuisine tunisienne.* Paris: Jacques Grancher, Editeur, 1977.

INDEX

TABLE OF EQUIVALENTS

THE EXACT EQUIVALENTS IN THE FOLLOWING TABLES HAVE

BEEN ROUNDED FOR CONVENIENCE.

US/UK

oz=ounce

lb=pound

in=inch

ft=foot

tbl=tablespoon

fl oz=fluid ounce

qt=quart

METRIC

g=gram

kg=kilogram

mm=millimeter

cm=centimeter

ml=milliliter

l=liter

WEIGHTS

US/UK	Metric
1 oz	30 g
2 oz	60 g
3 oz	90 g
4 oz (¼ lb)	125 g
5 oz (⅓ lb)	155 g
6 oz	185 g
7 oz	220 g
8 oz (½ lb)	250 g
10 oz	315 g
12 oz (¾ lb)	375 g
14 oz	440 g
16 oz (1 lb)	500 g
1½ lb	750 g
2 lb	1 kg
3 lb	1.5 kg

OVEN TEMPERATURES

Fahrenheit	Celsius	Gas
250	20	½
275	140	1
300	150	2
325	160	3
350	180	4
375	190	5
400	200	6
425	220	7
450	230	8
475	240	9
500	260	10

LIQUIDS

US	Metric	UK
2 tbl	30 ml	1 fl oz
¼ cup	60 ml	2 fl oz
⅓ cup	80 ml	3 fl oz
½ cup	125 ml	4 fl oz
⅔ cup	160 ml	5 fl oz
¾ cup	180 ml	6 fl oz
1 cup	250 ml	8 fl oz
1½ cups	75 ml	12 fl oz
2 cups	500 ml	16 fl oz
4 cups/1 qt	1 l	32 fl oz

LENGTH MEASURES

⅛ in	3 mm
¼ in	6 mm
½ in	12 mm
1 in	2.5 cm
2 in	5 cm
3 in	7.5 cm
4 in	10 cm
5 in	13 cm
6 in	15 cm
7 in	18 cm
8 in	20 cm
9 in	23 cm
10 in	25 cm
11 in	28 cm
12 in/1 ft	30 cm

All-purpose (plain) flour/ dried bread crumbs/chopped nuts

¼ cup	1 oz	30 g
⅓ cup	1½ oz	45 g
½ cup	2 oz	60 g
¾ cup	3 oz	90 g
1 cup	4 oz	125 g
1½ cups	6 oz	185 g
2 cups	8 oz	250 g

Whole-Wheat (Wholemeal) Flour

3 tbl	1 oz	30 g
½ cup	2 oz	60 g
⅔ cup	3 oz	90 g
1 cup	4 oz	125 g
1¼ cups	5 oz	155 g
1⅔ cups	7 oz	210 g
1¾ cups	8 oz	250 g

Brown Sugar

¼ cup	1½ oz	45 g
½ cup	3 oz	90 g
¾ cup	4 oz	125 g
1 cup	5½ oz	170 g
1½ cups	8 oz	250 g
2 cups	10 oz	315 g

White Sugar

¼ cup	2 oz	60 g
⅓ cup	3 oz	90 g
½ cup	4 oz	125 g
¾ cup	6 oz	185 g
1 cup	8 oz	250 g
1½ cups	12 oz	375 g
2 cups	1 lb	500 g

Raisins/Currants/Semolina

¼ cup	1 oz	30 g
⅓ cup	2 oz	60 g
½ cup	3 oz	90 g
¾ cup	4 oz	125 g
1 cup	5 oz	155 g

Long-Grain Rice/Cornmeal

⅓ cup	2 oz	60 g
½ cup	2½ oz	75 g
¾ cup	4 oz	125 g
1 cup	5 oz	155 g
1½ cups	8 oz	250 g

Dried Beans

¼ cup	1½ oz	45 g
⅓ cup	2 oz	60 g
½ cup	3 oz	90 g
¾ cup	5 oz	155 g
1 cup	6 oz	185 g
1¼ cups	8 oz	250 g
1½ cups	12 oz	375 g

Rolled Oats

⅓ cup	1 oz	30 g
⅔ cup	2 oz	60 g
1 cup	3 oz	90 g
1½ cups	4 oz	125 g
2 cups	5 oz	155 g

Jam/Honey

2 tbl	2 oz	60 g
¼ cup	3 oz	90 g
½ cup	5 oz	155 g
¾ cup	8 oz	250 g
1 cup	11 oz	345 g

Grated Parmesan/Romano Cheese

¼ cup	1 oz	30 g
½ cup	2 oz	60 g
¾ cup	3 oz	90 g
1 cup	4 oz	125 g
1⅓ cups	5 oz	155 g
2 cups	7 oz	220 g